I0099340

CHILDREN'S EDITION OF TOUCHING INCIDENTS AND REMARKABLE ANSWERS TO PRAYER

by
S.B. Shaw

Author of
Touching Incidents and Remarkable Answers to Prayer
The Dying Testimonies of Saved and Unsaved

SCHMUL PUBLISHING COMPANY
NICHOLASVILLE, KENTUCKY

This Schmul Publishing Co. edition is not a scanned facsimile of a used book. It has not been "updated" or edited into modern English, punctuation or grammar, but is accurate to the author's own style and usage. The text has been carefully proofread for accuracy and formatted for easier reading by today's readers. Every effort has been made to prevent disordered text.

Published by Schmul Publishing Co.
PO Box 776
Nicholasville, KY 40340
USA

ISBN 10: 0-88019-637-8
ISBN 13: 978-0-88019-637-6

Visit us on the Internet at www.wesleyanbooks.com, or order direct from the publisher by calling 800-772-6657, or by writing to the above address.

In Jesus forever

A. B. Shaw

Your loving friend.
Mrs. S. B. Shaw,

Contents

Publisher's Preface

Solomon Benjamin Shaw was converted in 1876, and entirely sanctified soon after. While holding credentials in the Methodist Episcopal Church, he labored as an evangelist across the broad spectrum of holiness churches, asserting that his was an "undenominational" ministry. In his testimony he said, "God honored my efforts, and from that day to this I have never held a meeting without seeing the fruit of my labor... I have been permitted to see thousands saved..."

He enlarged the reach of his ministry by authoring and publishing several books. Following the success of *Touching Incidents and Remarkable Answers to Prayer*, he compiled the last words and testimonies of saints and sinners in *The Dying Testimonies of Saved and Unsaved*, and responded to the urging of his reading public with this volume, *Children's Edition of Touching Incidents and Remarkable Answers to Prayer*.

One can discern his intent within the first few pages. With many ennobling tales, it also presents cautionary and moral stories, intended to urge young people to commit their hearts to Christ and holy living, no matter the personal cost, to find their home at last with their Savior in Heaven.

Ostensibly written for young readers, parents will find these stories good bedtime reading, but preachers and teachers will also discover a plentiful supply of illustrations for sermons, Sunday School and vacation bible school lessons.

—D. CURTIS HALE
Publisher, 2021

Prefatory Note.

FOR MANY YEARS in our work among children, we have felt the need of something similar to this book.

The eagerness with which they have read the larger work or listened to its reading by others has increased our desire to supply them with something similar yet more especially adapted to their need, and at a price that would bring it easily within reach. This book is the result. Like the larger edition it will speak for itself. All know that children like pictures but we fear very few realize how lasting is the impression they make upon the minds and hearts. Pictures that awaken foolish, impure or unkind thoughts have a tendency to poison the mind and destroy the soul forever. On the other hand, the pictures in this book will suggest thoughts of God and heaven and awaken desires to live pure lives which will sooner or later result in the salvation of many of our young readers. The impressions made on the mind for good can never be erased.

The cuts are new and made especially for this work.

We pray that multitudes may have the privilege of reading this book and that all readers will find the way to God and a home in heaven. Let all that appreciate the good the book will do help us circulate it. God bless all our readers.

Your brother in Jesus forever,
S. B. SHAW
Grand Rapids, Mich., May 11, 1895.

Introduction.

DEAR CHILDREN:—Mr. Shaw has told you how he came to write this book. We are sure it will interest you for children (and most older people too) like stories; especially good and true stories like these. In all of these we have selected there are precious lessons of kindness and sympathy and obedience and gratitude and courage, and faithfulness; and then there are two other very important lessons which I wish you to learn. The first is that children can be and should be true Christians, that is, have their sins forgiven for Jesus' sake and their hearts changed so that they love God and the right and hate every thing that is wrong. The second lesson is that we must be Christians to be ready to live or ready to die. A great many people seem to think that the only reason we need to be good is that we may be ready to die. You will find in this book several accounts of happy deaths of Christian children, but you will, if you notice, find also much that tells of the good done by happy Christian children that lived. Next to being saved ourselves the best thing in all the world is to be the means of doing good to others and getting others saved. And this work that is the grandest that any man or woman can do, you can do also if your hearts are filled with God's love. Let me tell you something I read a short time ago concerning Alfred Cookman, one of the most devoted men the world has ever known. He was converted when only ten years old. About his conversion he said: "I shall never forget the 12th of February, 1838—the birthday of my eternal life." But what especially attracted my attention was this statement: "*The year after his conversion there were gathered at one time in his father's house forty children who had been brought to Christ mainly through his efforts.*" Wasn't that wonderful and must he not have been a happy boy? Some folks have an idea that good children nearly always die young, but that is a big mistake; it is one of the thoughts that Satan suggests to keep children from giving their hearts to God. The fact is that most older people who are Christians were converted when they were young and Alfred Cookman lived many years and won a great many souls. His last words were, "I am sweeping through the gates, washed in the blood of the Lamb." What a blessed life and what a glorious death! The song "Sweeping through the Gates," was written in memory of his dying testimony.

I hope that many Christian workers who will go out "after their thousands for Jesus" may be found among you who read this book and that every one of you may learn that which will help you to live happy, earnest, useful Christian lives.

Your loving friend,
Mrs. S. B. Shaw.
Grand Rapids, Mich., May 11, 1895.

Always Tell the Truth.—Be True.

TRUTHFULNESS IS A MARK of Christianity. The heathen go astray, speaking lies as soon as they are born. In China a mother will give her boy a reward for the best falsehood that he can tell. Beginning so early, and regarding it such a fine thing to tell wrong stories, they become skillful in falsehoods. Some parents in Christian America are very careless in this matter. It made my heart ache one day when I saw a lady in a street car trying to keep her little boy awake by telling him that, if he went to sleep, that man who had all those teeth in his window (referring to a dentist's office they had passed) would come into the car and pull every tooth out of his mouth. The little fellow looked up dreadfully scared, and did his best to keep awake; but I thought to myself, when he finds out what a wrong story his mother has told, he will not believe her even when she tells the truth. He will be like a little fellow of whom I heard once, whose mother told him that if he went to play in a bank from which the men had been drawing sand for building, a bear would come out and eat him up. One day another boy tried to coax him to go there and play, but he said, no, he was afraid of the bears. The other boy said there were no bears. "But there be bears cause my mother said there be bears." While they were disputing the minister happened to come along, and they asked him if there were bears in the sand-bank. He told them there were none. "But," said the first little boy, "my mother said there be bears there." "I am sorry she said so," said the minister, "but the truth is, there are none." The child began to cry, and started for home as fast as he could go. "O mamma!" he said, "Did you tell me a wrong story?

Did you tell me there be bears down at the sand-bank when there ben't any?" She saw what a dreadful sin she had committed, and she told him that she was sorry; but she was afraid that if he played there he would get buried in the sand, and she told him that to keep him away. "But, mamma, it is such an awful thing to tell a wrong story." "I know it Tommy, I know it," she said, tears coming into her eyes; "and we will ask Jesus to forgive me, and I will never do it again." They knelt down, and she was just about to pray when he said, "Wait, mamma; let me ask him; maybe you won't tell him truly." That pierced her heart like a dagger. She saw that her little boy had lost confidence in her truthfulness even when she prayed. — JENNIE FOWLER WILLING, in *A Dozen Be's for Boys*.

The Child-Heroine of New Brunswick.

We have read a touching incident about three little children, who, last autumn, late in the season, wandered alone in a dreary region of New Brunswick. The sun had already sunk in the west, and the gloom of evening was spreading itself over the surrounding country.

The night came on fast; and feeling sure that they could not get home before daybreak, the eldest (a girl of only six years) quietly placed the two little ones in a sheltered nook on the sea-beach; and fearing the cold chilly night for the younger children, Mary stripped off most of her own clothes to keep them warm.

She then started off to gather dry sea-weed, and whatever else she could find, to cover them with. Having tenderly in this way wrought for some time to make them a nest, she at last fell down exhausted with the cold, and half bare to the cold inclement night.

That evening the loving father and tender mother sat up wondering at their children's long absence; the hours dragged slowly past with anxious watching and silent listening for the well-known little pattering feet. In vain the fond parents' eyes pierced through the darkness. At length they roused the neighbors with their anxious inquiries after their lost ones. All that night was passed in searching and in tears, till early in the morning, lying fast asleep and somewhat numbed with cold, were found little Johnny and Lizzie. But, oh! a touching spectacle lay near them; their young savior was stiff, cold, and dead on the sea-weed which the poor little child-heroine had not strength to drag into the nook, where those she so deeply loved, and died to save, were sleeping. Thus this little New Brunswick girl died in her successful and self-sacrificing endeavor to save her brother and sister.

Does not this recall the love of the Lord Jesus Christ to you who read? Mary went to the full extent of human love in dying for her little brother and sister. "Greater love hath no man than this, that a man lay down his life for his friends." Yet the Lord Jesus laid down his life for his enemies; for "scarcely for a righteous man will one die; yet peradventure for a good man some would even dare to die; but God commendeth His love toward us," etc. He makes no mistakes. Yet how many listen to this story with more emotion and interest than they do to the story of the cross, where the love of Jesus, the Son of God, is told in letters of blood! — *Dawn of the Morning.*

Annie and Vanie's First Real Prayer.

Two sisters, one about five years of age, the other one older, were accustomed to go each Saturday morning, some distance from home, to get chips and shavings from a cooper shop.

One morning, with basket well filled, they were returning home when the elder one was taken suddenly sick with cramps or cholera. She was in great pain, and unable to proceed, much less to bear the basket home. She sat down on the basket, and the younger one held her from falling.

The street was a lonely one, occupied by workshops, factories, etc. Every one was busy within; not a person was seen on the street.

The little girls were at a loss what to do. Too timid to go into any workshop, they sat a while, as silent and quiet as the distressing pains would allow.

Soon the elder girl said: "You know, Annie, that a good while ago mother told us that if we ever got into trouble, we should pray and God would help us. Now you help me to get down upon my knees, and hold me up, and we will pray."

There on the side-walk did these two little children ask God to send some one to help them home.

The simple and brief prayer being ended, the sick girl was again helped up, and sat on the basket, waiting the answers to their prayers.

Presently Annie saw, far down the street on the opposite side, a man come out from a factory, look around him up and down the street and go back into the factory.

"O sister, he has gone in again," said Annie. "Well," said Vanie, "perhaps he is not the one God is going to send. If he is, he will come back again."

"There he comes again," said Annie. "He walks this way. He seems looking for something. He walks slow, and is without his hat. He puts his hand to his head, as if he did not know what to do. O sister, he has gone in again; what shall we do?"

"That may not be the one whom God will send to help us," said Vanie. "If he is, he will come out again."

"Oh yes, there he is; this time with his hat on," said Annie. "He comes this way; he walks slowly looking around on every side. He does not see us; perhaps the trees hide us. Now he sees us, and is coming quickly."

A brawny German in broken accent asks:

"O children, what is the matter?"

"O sir," said Annie, "sister here is so sick she cannot walk, and we cannot get home."

"Where do you live, my dear?"

"At the end of this street; you can see the house from here."

"Never mind," said the man, "I takes you home."

So the strong man gathered the sick child in his arms, and with her head pillowed upon his shoulder, carried her to the place pointed out by the younger girl. Annie ran around the house to tell her mother that there was a man at the front door wishing to see her. The astonished mother, with a mixture of surprise and joy, took charge of the precious burden and the child was laid upon a bed.

After thanking the man, she expected him to withdraw, but instead, he stood turning his hat in his hands as one who wishes to say something, but knows not how to begin.

The mother observing this, repeated her thanks and finally said: "Would you like me to pay you for bringing my child home?"

"O no," said he with tears, "God pays me! God pays me! I would like to tell you something, but I speak English so poorly that I fear you will not understand."

The mother assured him that she was used to the German and could understand him very well.

"I am the proprietor of an ink factory," said he. "My men work by the piece. I have to keep separate accounts with each. I pay them every Saturday. At twelve o'clock they will be at my desk for their money. This week I have had many hindrances and was behind with my books. I was working hard at them with the sweat on my face, in my great anxiety to be ready in time. Suddenly I could not see the figures; the words in the book all ran together, and I had a plain impression on my mind that some one in the street wished to see me. I went out, looked up and down the street, but seeing no one, went back to my desk and wrote a little. Presently the darkness was greater than before, and the impression stronger than before, that someone in the street needed me.

"Again I went out, looked up and down the street, walked a little way, puzzled to know what I meant. Was my hard work and were the cares of business driving me out of my wits? Unable to solve the mystery I turned again into my shop and to my desk.

"This time my fingers refused to grasp the pen. I found myself unable to write a word, or make a figure; but the impression was stronger than ever on my mind, that some-one needed my help. A voice seemed to say: 'Why don't you go out as I tell you? There is need of your help.' This time I took my hat on going out, resolved to stay till I found out whether I was losing my senses, or there was a duty for me to do. I walked some distance without seeing anyone, and was more and more puzzled, till I came opposite the children, and found that there was indeed need of my help. I cannot understand it, madam."

As the noble German was about leaving the house, the younger girl had the courage to say: "O mother, we prayed."

Thus the mystery was solved, and with tear-stained cheeks, a heaving breast, and a humble, grateful heart, the kind man went back to his accounts.

I have enjoyed many a happy hour in conversation with Annie in her own house since she has a home of her own. The last I knew of Annie and Vanie, they were living in the same city, earnest Christian women. Their children were growing up around them, who, I hope, will have like confidence in mother, and faith in God.   JEIGH ARRH.

Annie was the wife of James A. Clayton, of San Jose, California. I have enjoyed their hospitality and esteem both very highly.   JAMES ROGERS, Of Alabama Conference, M. E. Church.

"Does This Railroad Lead to Heaven?"

In traveling we often meet with persons of different nationalities and languages; we also meet with incidents of various character, some sorrowful, others, joyful and instructive. One of the latter character I witnessed recently while traveling upon the cars. The train was going west and the time was evening. At a station a little girl about eight years old came aboard, carrying a budget under her arm. She came into the car and deliberately took a seat. She then commenced an eager scrutiny of faces, but all were strange to her. She appeared weary, and placing her budget for a pillow, she prepared to try and secure a little sleep. Soon the conductor came along collecting tickets and fare. Observing him she asked him if she might lie there. The gentlemanly conductor replied that she might, and then kindly asked for her ticket. She informed him that she had none, when the following conversation ensued. Said the conductor:

"Where are you going?"

"I am going to heaven," she answered.

"Who pays your fare?" he asked again.

She then said, "Mister, does this railroad lead to heaven, and does Jesus travel on it?"

"I think not," he answered. "Why did you think so?"

"Why sir, before my ma died she used to sing to me of a heavenly railroad, and you looked so nice and kind that I thought this was the road. My ma used to sing of Jesus on the heavenly railroad, and that He paid the fare for everybody, and that the train stopped at every station to take people on board; but my ma don't sing to me any more. Nobody sings to me now; and I thought I'd take the cars and go to ma. Mister, do you sing to your little girl about the railroad that goes to heaven? You have a little girl, haven't you?"

He replied, weeping, "No, my little dear, I have no little girl now. I had one once; but she died some time ago, and went to heaven."

"Did she go over this railroad, and are you going to see her now?" she asked.

By this time every person in the coach was upon their feet, and most of them were weeping. An attempt to describe what I witnessed is almost futile. Some said: "God bless the little girl." Hearing some person say that she was an angel, the little girl earnestly replied: "Yes, my ma used to say that I would be an angel some time."

Addressing herself once more to the conductor, she asked him, "Do you love Jesus? I do, and if you love Him, He will let you ride to heaven on His railroad. I am going there and I wish you would go with me. I know Jesus will let me into heaven when I get there and He will let you in, too, and everybody that will ride on His railroad — yes, all these people. Wouldn't you like to see heaven and Jesus, and your little girl?"

These words, so pathetically and innocently uttered, brought a great gush of tears from all eyes, but most profusely from those of the conductor. Some who were traveling on the heavenly railroad shouted aloud for joy.

She now asked the conductor: "Mister, may I lie here until we get to heaven?"

"Yes, dear, yes," he answered.

"Will you wake me up then, so that I may see my ma, and your little girl and Jesus?" she asked, "for I do so much want to see them all."

The answer came in broken accents, but in words very tenderly spoken: "Yes, dear angel, yes. God bless you."

"Amen!" was sobbed by more than a score of voices.

Turning her eyes again upon the conductor, she interrogated him again: "What shall I tell your little girl when I see her? Shall I tell her that I saw her pa on Jesus' railroad? Shall I?"

This brought a fresh flood of tears from all present, and the conductor knelt by her side, and, embracing her wept the reply he could not utter. At this juncture the brakeman called out: "H—s." The conductor arose and requested him to attend to his (the conductor's) duty at the station, for he was engaged. That was a precious place. I thank God that I was a witness to this scene, but I was sorry that at this point I was obliged to leave the train.

We learn from this incident that out of the mouths of even babes God hath ordained strength, and that we ought to be willing to represent the cause of our blessed Jesus even in a railroad coach.

The Sequel

REV. DOSH: I wish to relieve my heart by writing to you, and saying that that angel visit on the cars was a blessing to me, although I did not realize it in its fullness until some hours after. But blessed be the Redeemer, I know now that I am His, and He is mine. I no longer wonder why Christians are happy. Oh, my joy, my joy! The instrument of my salvation has gone to God. I had purposed adopting her in the place of my little daughter, who is now in heaven. With this intention I took her to C——b, and on my return trip I took her back to S——n, where she left the cars. In consultation with my wife in regard to adopting her, she replied, "Yes, certainly, and immediately too, for there is a Divine providence in this. Oh," said she, "I could never refuse to take under my charge the instrument of my husband's salvation."

I made inquiry for the child at S——n and learned that in three days after her return she died suddenly, without any apparent disease, and her happy soul had gone to dwell with her ma, my little girl, and the angels in heaven. I was sorry to hear of her death but my sorrow is turned to joy when I think my angel-daughter received intelligence from earth concerning her pa, and that he is on the heavenly railway. Oh! sir, me thinks I see her near the Redeemer. I think I hear her sing: "I'm safe at home, and pa and ma are coming;" and I find myself sending back the reply: "Yes, my darling, we are coming and will soon be there." Oh, my dear sir, I am glad that I ever formed your acquaintance; may the blessing of the great God rest upon you. Please write to me, and be assured, I would be most happy to meet you again.—*Rev. J. M. Dosh, in Christian Expositor.*

Willie Court—The Patient Christian Sufferer.

The following touching account of the life and death of this little Christian hero is condensed from articles in the CHRISTIAN HOME of March 31, 1893, published at Council Bluffs, Iowa.

"In the year 1884, Willie's father, who was a miner, living with his wife and family in Leadville, Colorado, was killed in a snow-slide in the mountains. The mother, overcome by the shock, lost her reason. She was sent to an asylum and there soon died. Jennie, then five, and Willie, then three years of age, were taken in charge by Christian women of Leadville, who wrote to us, appealing in their behalf. As in all cases, we wrote back that we would gladly receive them in the Master's name. The two children, Jennie and Willie, were sent to us in May, 1885. Jennie was then six and Willie four years of age. Jennie was and is a healthy child; but Willie was deformed, afflicted with curvature of the spine. During the first three years that he was with us, he was able at times to play about, always too prone to play violently, requiring constant watching. Often he would stop short in his play, doubled up with excruciating pain, and would have to be carried into the house. Then a terrible abscess formed in his groin, and from that time he was a confirmed invalid, seldom able to leave his bed. We had consultations of the best physicians of Council Bluffs and Omaha—physicians as good as there are in the land. They all pronounced his case hopeless.

Spiritually his case was a wonder of an exceptional nature. When he came to us, he was of a very repulsive nature, disobedient, cross, treacherous. It seemed hard to punish him because he was so delicate, and hence his case appeared almost hopeless. But finally, the workers made him a special object of prayer, and strove, with peculiar tenderness and earnestness, to lead him to Jesus. God blessed our efforts, and one day he exclaimed, "I *do* love Jesus and I *will* be good." Then we all rejoiced with exceeding great joy, praying to God to keep him and perfect in him the good work begun by the Spirit. Glory be to the name of God, we have every reason to believe that the child, at that time six years old, was truly regenerated. We never witnessed a greater change in mortal. Before he was selfish. From that blessed moment, he was ready to give up any sweetmeat or toy, no matter how highly treasured, to his playmates. Before, he was peevish, cross, disobedient. After that time he was happy, obedient, patient, just a precious little saint…

"He made the Home workers more patient and loving. He blessed all who saw him. He brought tears to eyes long accustomed to look on suffering without being moved. When the doctors were here to perform an operation, he bore it all without complaint, and took nothing to deaden the pain. When the operation was completed, he looked up gratefully and said: "Thank you, doctors!" There were men in the room used to scenes of suffering, but not one of those stout hearts but turned to brush away a tear.

"Not only this but the Lord saw fit to make of dear

The above is reproduced from Willie's photo.

little Willie McCourt the means of much good to thousands of His children, leading the afflicted to bear their affliction with more patience, and all Christians to realize, more sensibly than ever before, that God doeth all things for our best good. Had we the space we could quote from scores of letters from all parts of the United States, from persons in all stations of life, such expressions as these:

"I have been greatly blessed in my Christian life by reading of the wonderful patience of dear little Willie."

"I have been afflicted for years, and have been too impatient. The account of what Jesus has done for Willie has been blessed to my soul."

At one time the following statement concerning him was made in a report of a visit to the Home, which was published in the *Omaha Daily World-Herald:*

"The Home has one little soul who is such a monument of suffering and patience as well as of precocious sanctity that he is usually mentioned before any other child in the institution. His name is Willie McCourt. His body is wrenched and twisted with pain. His back has sores which never heal. He has undergone operations that the veteran of many battles might well have shrunk from. It is impossible for him to lie on his back. He lies day and night face downward on a pile of pillows. His head is dispropotionately large, his face most piteous with suffering, but his eyes are alight with ecstacy such as must have been in the eyes of the little ones who left the Rhineland six centuries ago to follow their sires to the crusades. Whatever is best in the Home is brought to this bed-side. If there is a picture book, it is placed on his counterpane. If there is a canary bird, it hangs above his bed. If there is a flower, it blooms in a window near. This extraordinary little sufferer looks forward to Heaven as most children do to next Christmas, and his name has gone broadcast."…

At last, after many years of intensest suffering, the Savior called, saying, "It is enough!" and Willie, beloved of Jesus, beloved of the Home, has gone to his reward. Friday night, February 24th, 1893, at 10:05. the spirit of the precious little one winged his flight to the Home above where pain and suffering will never more be known.

Dear Willie was conscious almost to the last breath. A short time before his death he said, "I'll soon be with Jesus!" and again, "I want to go to Jesus!" He died surrounded by the Home workers and many of the older children of the Home, a sorrowing band, yet rejoicing that the precious little saint was free.

Little Willie has been a great burden. With him the Home workers have spent countless sleepless nights in the past five years. For hours at a time one or another of them has held the patient little sufferer in their arms. Once every day and often many times, his sores, more offensive than tongue can tell, have been dressed. But all this has been borne with joy and our arms now ache for the little, helpless form, while we still rejoice that he is at rest in the arms of Jesus. Willie has been with us nearly eight years. He, with all his suffering and all the labor he cost, was the light and joy of us all. He strengthened our faith and led us nearer to the cross. Praise God that He gave him into our care and permitted us, in ministering to him, to minister to the Lord and Savior. His memory is a precious legacy. Little Willie, patient sufferer, Christian hero, farewell until that day when we meet in the Father's Home above!

As was fitting, little Willie's funeral was one of the most largely attended, and one of the most remarkable, ever held in this city. All the daily papers of this city and Omaha wrote feelingly in regard to it, and his life and character. Below we give the account published in the daily *Nonpareil* the 28th of February:

"The large auditorium of Broadway M. E. church was filled last Sunday afternoon at three o'clock on the occasion of the funeral of Willie McCourt, the little Christian hero, who died at the Christian Home, last Friday night, a sketch of whose remarkable life and character was given in *The Nonpareil* of a recent issue.

"The exercises were of a most impressive character. At three o'clock the casket bearing the precious remains was borne up the aisle by six of the Home boys, who acted as pall-bearers. The casket was followed by about one hundred more of the Home workers and children, for whom seats had been reserved in the front of the church. As the procession moved up the aisle the organist played a funeral march, and the deep solemnity of the scene was one never to be forgotten by those who were present. The floral offerings by the Home workers and admiring friends of the city were elaborate. Beside many elegant designs little Willie literally rested in a bed of flowers.

"The exercises were conducted by the Rev. Mr. Dudley, pastor of the Broadway M. E. church, the Rev. T. F. Thickstun, pastor of the Berean Baptist church, the Rev. C. W. Brewer, pastor of the Fifth Avenue M. E. church, and the Rev. J. G. Lemen, manager of the Home. All testified to the wonderful faith and Christian heroism during years of intense suffering of little Willie, who was but twelve years of age. For years he had lain face downward, not knowing what it was to be free from pain. Yet during all that time no complaint escaped his lips. When asked how he was, his answer always was: 'I am all right,' or 'I am better,' when it was plain to see that he was at that moment racked with pain in every limb. He was always ready to talk of Jesus, and conversed with the old and with the ministers of the Gospel in a way to instruct and edify. His fame has gone out to all parts of the United States.

"That a little homeless boy, only twelve years of age,

should attract to his funeral such a concourse of people, from this city and from Omaha, as was in attendance, is indeed remarkable, and is a striking evidence of the fact that there is no power in the world that attracts men like a Living Faith in the Christ, be that faith displayed by young or old. Little Willie has gone, but the memory of his heroic life will be treasured at the Home, and by thousands of Christians in this city and the nation at large for all the years to come."

From a very large number of sympathizing letters received from the friends of the Home in all parts of the land, we give the following sample extracts:

"We were sad to hear of the death of dear Willie McCourt, for by his patience and Christ-like character he had endeared himself to us. He has heard the Voice saying, 'Come, ye blessed of my Father,' and has entered into rest."

"My tears fell as I read that the life of dear Willie McCourt had been transferred from the clay tabernacle which had been so full of suffering to the Heavenly Home. For him all agony of earth is finished, but the work which under God he began still goes on. The influence of his life will never be ended."

"What a sermon to the children is contained in Willie's conversion and his subsequent life. Jesus delights to save children. Tell the children of Willie; and by his life be encouraged, as never before, to labor to bring your little ones to Him who will take them in His arms of everlasting love."

The Young Martyr.

On the afternoon of August 9, 1853, a little Norwegian boy, named Kund Iverson, who lived in the city of Chicago, Ill., was going to the pastures for his cow, as light-hearted, I suppose, as boys usually are when going to the pasture on a summer afternoon. He came at length to a

The cries of the drowning child grew fainter and fainter.

stream of water, where there was a gang of idle, ill-looking, big boys, who, when they saw Kund, came up to him, and said they wanted him to go into Mr. Elston's garden and steal some apples.

"No," said Kund promptly; "I cannot steal, I am sure."

"Well, but you've got to," they cried.

They threatened to duck him, for these wicked big boys had often frightened little boys into robbing gardens for them. Little boys, they thought, were less likely to get found out.

The threat did not frighten Kund, so, to make their words good, they seized him and dragged him into the river, and, in spite of his cries and struggles, plunged him in. But the heroic boy even with the water gurgling and choking in his throat, never flinched, for he knew that God had said: "Thou shalt not steal," and God's law he had made his law; and no cursing, or threats, or cruelty of the big boys would make him give up. Provoked by his firmness, I suppose, they determined to see if they could conquer him. So they ducked him again but it still was, "No, no;" and they kept him under water. Was there no one near to hear his distressing cries, and rescue the poor child from their cruel grip? No; there was none to rescue him; and gradually the cries of the drowning child grew fainter and fainter, and his struggles less and less, and the boy was drowned. He could die, but would not steal.

A German boy who had stood near, much frightened by what he saw, ran home to tell the news. The agonized parents hastened to the spot, and all night they searched for the lifeless body of their lost darling. It was found the next morning; and who shall describe their feelings as they clasped the little form to their bosoms? Early piety had blossomed in his little life. He loved his Bible and his Saviour. His seat was never vacant at Sunday school, and so intelligent, conscientious and steadfast had he been, that it was expected he would soon be received into the church of his parents.

Perhaps the little boy used often to think how, when he grew up, he would like to be a preacher or a missionary, and do something for his Lord and Master. He did not know what post he might be called to occupy, even as a little child; and, as he left home that afternoon and looked his last look in his mother's face, he thought he was only going after his cow; and other boys, and the neighbors, if they saw him, thought so too. They did not then know that instead of going to the pasture, he was going to preach one of the most powerful sermons of Bible law and Bible principles the country ever heard. They did not know that he was going to give an example of steadfastness of purpose and of unflinching integrity, such as should thrill the heart of this nation with wonder and admiration. He was then only a Norwegian boy, Kund Iverson, only thirteen years old, but his name was soon to be reckoned with martyrs and heroes. And as the story of his moral heroism winged its way from state to state, and city to city, and village to village, how many mothers cried with full hearts: "May his spirit rest upon my boy!" And strong men have wept over it and exclaimed: "God be praised for the lad!" And rich men put their hands into their pockets, and said, "Let us build him a monument; let his name be perpetuated, for his memory is blessed." May there be a generation of Kund Iversons, strong in their integrity, true to their Bibles, ready to die rather than do wrong. — *The Cynosure*

A Child's Prayer Answered.

The following touching incident, which drew tears from my eyes, was related to me a short time since, by a dear friend who had it from an eyewitness of the same. It occurred in the great city of New York, on one of the coldest days in February.

A little boy about ten years old was standing before a shoe-store in Broadway, barefooted, peering through the window, and shivering with cold.

A lady riding up the street in a beautiful carriage, drawn by horses finely caparisoned, observed the little fellow in his forlorn condition, and immediately ordered the driver to draw up and stop in front of the store. The lady, richly dressed in silk, alighted from her carriage, went quickly to the boy, and said:

"My little fellow, why are you looking so earnestly in that window?"

"I was asking God to give me a pair of shoes," was the reply. The lady took him by the hand and went into the store, and asked the proprietor if he would allow one of his clerks to go and buy half a dozen pairs of stockings for the boy. He readily assented. She then asked him if he could give her a basin of water and a towel, and he replied: "Certainly," and quickly brought them to her.

She took the little fellow to the back part of the store, and, removing her gloves, knelt down, washed those little feet and dried them with the towel.

By this time the young man had returned with the stockings. Placing a pair upon his feet, she purchased and gave him a pair of shoes, and tying up the remaining pairs of stockings, gave them to him, and patting him on the head said: "I hope my little fellow, that you now feel more comfortable."

As she turned to go, the astonished lad caught her hand, and looking up in her face, with tears in his eyes answered her question with these words: "Are you God's wife?" — *Parish Register*.

The Converted Infidel.

Some two miles from the village of C., on a road that wound in among the hills, stood a great white house. It was beautifully situated upon a gentle slope facing the south, and overlooking a most charming landscape. Away in the distance, a mountain lifted itself against the clear blue sky. At its base rolled a broad, deep river. Nestling down in the beautiful valley that intervened, reposed the charming little village, with its neat cottages, white church, little red school-house, and one or two mansions that told of wealth. Here and there in the distance a pond was visible; while farm houses and humbler dwellings dotted the picture in every direction.

Such was the home of three promising children, who, for the last three months, had been constant members of the village Sabbath-school. The eldest was a girl of some fourteen years. John, the second, was a bright, amiable lad of eleven. The other, the little rosy-cheeked, laughing

Ella, with her golden curls and sunny smile, had just gathered the roses of her ninth summer.

The father of these interesting children was the rich Captain Lowe. He was a man of mark, such, in many respects, as are often found in rural districts. Strictly moral, intelligent and well read, kind-hearted and naturally benevolent, he attracted all classes of community to himself, and wielded great influence in his town.

But, not withstanding all these excellences, Mr. Lowe was an *infidel*. He ridiculed, in his good-natured way, the idea of prayer, looked upon conversion as a solemn farce, and believed the most of professing Christians were well-meaning but deluded people. He was well versed in all the subtle arguments of infidel writers, had studied the Bible quite carefully, and could argue against it in the most plausible manner. Courteous and kind to all, few could be offended at his frank avowal of infidel principles, or resent his keen, half-jovial sarcasms upon the peculiarities of some weak-minded, though sincere members of the church.

But Mr. Lowe saw and acknowledged the saving influence of the *morality* of Christianity. He had, especially, good sense enough to confess that the Sabbath-school was a noble moral enterprise. He was not blind to the fact, abundantly proved by all our criminal records, that few children trained under her influences ever grow up to vice and crime. Hence his permission for his children to attend the Sabbath-school.

Among the many children who kneeled as penitents at the altar in the little vestry, one bright, beautiful Sabbath, were Sarah Lowe and her brother and sister. It was a moving sight to see that gentle girl, with a mature thoughtfulness far beyond her years, take that younger brother and sister by the hand, and kneel with them at the mercy-seat—a sight to heighten the joy of angels.

When the children had told their mother what they

had done, and expressed a determination to try to be Christians, she, too, was greatly moved. She had been early trained in the principles and belief of Christianity, and had never renounced her early faith. Naturally confiding, with a yielding, conciliatory spirit, she had never obtruded her sentiments upon the notice of her husband, nor openly opposed any of his peculiar views. But now, when her little ones gathered around her and spoke of their new love for the Savior, their joy, and peace, and hope, she wept. All the holy influences of her own childhood and youth seemed breathing upon her heart. She remembered the faithful sermons of the old pastor whose hands had baptized her. She remembered, too, the family altar, and the prayers which were offered morning and evening by her sainted father. She remembered the counsels of her good mother, now in heaven. All these memories came crowding back upon her, and under their softening influences she almost felt herself a child again.

When Mr. Lowe first became aware of the change in his children, he was sorely puzzled to know what to do. He had given his consent for them to attend the Sabbath-school, and should he now be offended because they had yielded to its influence? Ought he not rather to have expected this? And, after all, would what they called religion make them any worse children? Though at first quite disturbed in his feelings, he finally concluded upon second thought to say nothing to them upon the subject, but to let things go on as usual.

But not so those happy young converts. They could not long hold their peace. They must tell their father also what they had experienced. Mr. Lowe heard them, but he made no attempt to ridicule their simple faith, as had been his usual course with others. They were *his* children, and none could boast of better. Still, he professed to see in their present state of mind nothing but youthful feeling, excited by the peculiar circumstances of the last few

It was a moving sight to see that gentle girl, take that younger brother and sister by the hand, and kneel with them at the mercy-seat— a sight to heighten the joy of angels.

weeks. But when they began in their childish ardor to exhort him also to seek the Lord, he checked their simple earnestness with a peculiar sternness which said to them: "The act must not be repeated."

The next Sabbath the father could not prevent a feeling of loneliness as he saw his household leave for church. The three children, with their mother, and Joseph, the hired boy, to drive and take care of the horse, all packed into the old commodious carriage, and started off. Never before had he such peculiar feelings as when he watched them slowly descending the hill.

To dissipate these emotions he took a dish of salt and started up the hill to a "mountain pasture" where his young cattle were enclosed for the season. It was a beautiful day in October, that queen month of the year. A soft melancholy breathed in the mild air of the mellow "Indian summer," and the varying hues of the surrounding forests, and the signs of decay seen upon every side, all combined to deepen the emotions which the circumstances of the morning had awakened.

His sadness increased; and as his path opened out into a bright, sunny spot far up on the steep hillside, he seated himself upon a mossy knoll and thought. Before him lay the beautiful valley, guarded on either side by its lofty hills, and watered by its placid river. It was a lovely picture; and as his eye rested upon the village, nestling down among its now gorgeous shade-trees and scarlet shrubbery, he could not help thinking of that company who were then gathered in the little church, with its spire pointing heavenward, nor of asking himself the question: "Why are they there?"

While thus engaged, his attention was attracted by the peculiar chirping of a ground-sparrow near by. He turned, and but a few feet from him he saw a large black snake, with its head raised about a foot above its body, which lay coiled upon the ground. Its jaws were distended, its forked tongue played around its open mouth, flashing in the sunlight like a small lambent flame, while its eyes were intently fixed upon the bird. There was a clear, sparkling light about those eyes that was fearful to behold — they fairly flashed with their peculiar bending fascination. The poor sparrow was fluttering around a circle of some few feet in diameter, the circle becoming smaller at each gyration of the infatuated bird. She appeared conscious of her danger, and yet unable to break the spell that bound her. Nearer and still nearer she fluttered her little wings to those open jaws; smaller and smaller

grew the circle, till at last, with a quick convulsive cry, she fell into the mouth of the snake.

As Mr. Lowe watched the bird, he became deeply interested in her fate. He started a number of times to destroy the reptile, and thus liberate the sparrow from her danger, but an unconquerable curiosity to see the end restrained him. All day long the scene just described was before him. He could not forget it nor dismiss it from his mind. The last cry of that poor little bird sinking into the jaws of death was constantly ringing in his ears, and the sadness of the morning increased.

Returning to his house, he seated himself in his library and attempted to read. What could be the matter? Usually he could command his thoughts at will, but now he could think of nothing but the scene on the mountain, or the little company in the house of God. Slowly passed the hours, and many times did he find himself, in spite of his resolution not to do so, looking down the road for the head of his dapple gray to emerge from the valley. It seemed a long time before the rumbling of the wheels was at length heard upon the bridge which crossed the mountain stream, followed in a few moments by the old carry-all creeping slowly up the hill.

The return of the family somewhat changed the course of his thoughts. They did not say anything to *him* about the good meeting they had enjoyed, and who had been converted since the last Sabbath; but they talked it all over among themselves, and how could he help hearing? He learned all about "how good farmer Haskell talked," and "how humble and devoted Esquire Wiseman appeared," and "how happy Benjamin and Samuel were;" though he seemed busy with his book and pretended to take no notice of what was said.

It was, indeed, true then that the old lawyer had become pious. He had heard the news before, but did not believe it. Now he had learned it as a fact. That strong-minded man, who had been a skeptic all his days, had ridiculed and opposed religion, was now a subject of "the children's revival." What could it mean? Was there something in religion after all? Could it be that what these poor fanatics, as he had always called them, said about the future world was correct? Was there a heaven, and a hell, and a God of justice? Were his darling children right, and was he alone wrong? Such were the thoughts of the boasted infidel, as he sat there listening to the half-whispered conversation of his happy children.

Little Ella came and climbed to her long accustomed place upon her father's knee, and throwing her arms around his neck, laid her glowing cheek, half-hidden by the clustering curls, against his own. He knew by her appearance she had something to say, but did not dare to say it. To remove this fear, he began to question her about her Sabbath-school. He inquired after her teacher, and who were her classmates, what she learned, etc. Gradually the shyness wore away, and the heart of the innocent praying child came gushing forth. She told him all that had been done that day— what her teacher had said of the prayer-meeting at noon, and who spoke, and how many went forward for prayers. Then folding her arms more closely around his neck, and kissing him tenderly, she added:

"Oh, father, I do wish you had been there!"

"Why do you wish I had been there, Ella?"

"Oh, just to see how happy Nellie Winslow looked while her grandfather was telling us children how much he loved the Savior, and how sorry he was that he did not give his heart to his heavenly Father when he was young. Then he laid his hand on Nellie's head, who was sitting by his side, and said: 'I thank God that he ever gave me a little praying granddaughter to lead me to the Savior.' And, father, I never in all my life saw anyone look so happy as Nellie did."

Mr. Lowe made no reply— how could he? Could he not see where the heart of his darling Ella was? Could he not see that by what she had told him about Esquire Wiseman and his pet Nellie, she meant *he* should understand how happy *she* should be if *her* father was a Christian? Ella had not said so in words—*that* was a forbidden subject— but the language of her earnest, loving look and manner was not to be mistaken; and the heart of the infidel father was deeply stirred. He kissed the rosy cheeks of the lovely girl, and taking his hat, left the house. He walked out into the field. He felt strangely. Before he was aware of the fact, he found his infidelity leaving him, and the simple, artless religion of childhood winning its way to his heart. Try as hard as he might, he could not help believing that his little Ella was a Christian. There was a reality about her simple faith and ardent love that was truly "the evidence of things not seen." What should he do? Should he yield to this influence and be led by his children to Christ? What! Captain Lowe, the boasted infidel overcome by the weakness of excited childhood! The thought roused his *pride* and with an exclamation of impatience at his folly, he suddenly wheeled about, and retracing his steps, with altered appearance, he re-entered his house.

His wife was alone, with an open Bible before her. As he entered he saw her hastily wipe away a tear. In passing her he glanced upon the open page, and his eye caught the words "YE MUST BE BORN AGAIN!" They went like an arrow to his heart. "TRUTH," said a voice within, with such fearful distinctness that he started at the fancied sound; and the influence which he had just supposed banished from his heart returned with ten-fold power. The strong man trembled. Leaving the sitting-room, he ascended the stairs to his chamber. Passing Sarah's room, a voice attracted his attention. It was the voice of prayer. He heard his own name pronounced, and he paused to listen.

"Oh, Lord, save my dear father. Lead him to the Savior. Let him see that he *must be born again*. Oh let not the *serpent charm him*! Save, oh, save my dear father!"

He could listen no longer, "*Let not the serpent charm him!*" And was he then like that helpless, little bird, who, fluttering around the head of the serpent, fell at last into

They came from their places of prayer, where they had lifted up their hearts to that God who had said: "Whatsoever ye shall ask the Father in my name he will give it you."

the jaws of death? The thought shot a wild torrent of newly awakened terror through his throbbing heart.

Hastening to his chamber he threw himself into a chair. He started! The voice of prayer again fell upon his ear. He listened. Yes, it was the clear, sweet accents of his little pet. Ella was praying — *was praying for him!*

"O Lord, bless my dear father. Make him a Christian, and may he and dear mother be prepared for heaven!"

Deeply moved, the father left the house and hastened to the barn. He would fain escape from those words of piercing power. They were like daggers in his heart. He entered the barn. Again he hears a voice. It comes from the hay-loft, in the rich silvery tones of his own noble boy. John had climbed up the ladder, and kneeling down upon the hay *was praying for his father*.

"O Lord, save my father!"

It was too much for the poor convicted man, and, rushing to the house he fell, sobbing upon his knees by the side of his wife and cried:

"O Mary, I am a poor, lost sinner! Our children are going to heaven, and I— I— *am going down to hell!* O Wife, is there mercy for a wretch like me?"

Poor Mrs. Lowe was completely overcome. She wept for joy. That her husband would ever be her companion in the way of holiness, she had never dared to hope. Yes, there was mercy for even them. "Come unto me, and find rest." Christ had said it, and her heart told her it was true. Together they would go to this loving Savior, and their little ones should show them the way.

The children were called in. They came from their places of prayer, where they had lifted up their hearts to that God who had said: *"Whatsoever ye shall ask the Father in my name he will give it you."* They had asked the Spirit's influence upon the hearts of their parents, and it had been granted. They gathered around their weeping, broken-hearted father and penitent mother, and pointed them to

the cross of Jesus. Long and earnestly they prayed, and wept and agonized. With undoubting trust in the promises, they waited at the mercy-seat, and their prayers were heard. Faith conquered. The Spirit came and touched these penitent hearts with the finger of love; and then sorrow was turned to joy—their night, dark and cheerless and gloomy, was changed to blessed day.

They arose from their knees, and Ella sprang to the arms of her father, and together they rejoiced in God.—*Rev. H. P. Andrews, in Christian Advocate.*

The Stowaway

On board an English steamer, a little ragged boy, aged nine years, was discovered on the fourth day of the voyage out from Liverpool to New York, and carried before the first mate, whose duty it was to deal with such cases. When questioned as to his object in being stowed away, and who had brought him on board, the boy, who had a beautiful sunny face, that looked like the very mirror of truth, replied that his step-father did it, because he could not afford to keep him nor pay his passage to Halifax where he had an aunt who was well off, and to whose house he was going.

The mate did not believe his story, in spite of the winning face and truthful accents of the boy. He had seen too much of stowaways to be easily deceived by them, he said; and it was his firm conviction that the boy had been brought on board and provided with food by the sailors.

The little fellow was very roughly handled in consequence. Day by day he was questioned and requestioned, but always with the same result. He did not know a sailor on board, and his father alone had secreted and given

him the food which he ate. At last the mate, wearied by the boy's persistence in the same story, and perhaps a little anxious to inculpate the sailors, seized him one day by the collar, and dragging him to the fore, told him that unless he told the truth, in ten minutes from that time he would hang from the yard-arm. He then made him sit under it on the deck. All around him were the passengers and sailors of the midway watch, and in front of him stood the inexorable mate, with chronometer in his hand, and the other officers of the ship by his side. It was a touching sight to see the pale, proud, scornful face of that noble boy; his head erect, his beautiful eyes bright through the tears that suffused them. When eight minutes had fled, the mate told him he had but two minutes to live, and advised him to speak the truth and save his life. But he replied with the utmost simplicity and sincerity, by asking the mate if he might pray. The mate said nothing, but nodded his head, and turned as pale as a ghost, and shook with trembling like a reed in the wind. And then all eyes turned on him, the brave and noble fellow—this poor boy whom society owned not, and whose own stepfather could not care for— knelt with clasped hands and eyes upturned to heaven.

There then occurred a scene as of Pentecost. Sobs broke from strong, hard hearts, as the mate sprang forward and clasped the boy to his bosom, and kissed him, and blessed him, and told him how sincerely he now believed his story and how glad he was that he had been brave enough to face death and be willing to sacrifice his life for the truth of his word.—*Illustrated Weekly Telegraph.*

The Golden Rule Exemplified

Early one morning while it was yet dark, a poor man came to my door and informed me that he had an infant child very sick, which he was afraid would die. He desired me to go to his home, and, if possible prescribe some medicine to relieve it. "For," said he, "I want to save its life, if possible." As he spoke thus his tears ran down his face. He then added:

"I am a poor man; but, doctor, I will pay you in work as much as you ask if you will go."

I said: "Yes, I will go with you as soon as I take a little refreshment."

"Oh, sir," said he, "I was going to try to get a bushel of corn, and get it ground to carry home, and I am afraid the child will die before I get there. I wish you would not wait for me;" and then he added: "We want to save the child's life if we can."

It being some miles to his house, I didn't arrive there until the sun was two hours high in the morning, when I found the mother holding her sick child, and six or seven little boys and girls around her, with clean hands and faces, looking as their mother did, lean and poor. On examining the sick child, I discovered that it was starving to death! I said to the mother: "You don't give milk enough for this child."

She said: "I suppose I don't."

"Well," said I, "you must feed it with milk."

She answered: "I would, sir, but I can't get any to feed it with."

I then said: "It will be well, then, for you to make a little water gruel, and feed your child."

To this she replied: "I was thinking I would if my husband brings home some Indian meal. He has gone to try to get some, and I am in hopes he will make out."

She said this with a sad countenance. I asked her with surprise: "Why, madam, have you not got anything to eat?"

She strove to suppress a tear, and answered sorrowfully: "No sir; we have had but little these some days."

I said: "What are your neighbors, that you should suffer among them?"

She said, "I suppose they are good people, but we are strangers in this place, and don't wish to trouble any of them, if we can get along without."

Wishing to give the child a little manna I asked for a spoon. The little girl went to the table drawer to get one, and her mother said to her: "Get the longest handled spoon." As she opened the drawer, I saw only two spoons, and both with handles broken off, but one handle was a little longer than the other. I thought to myself this is a very poor family, but I will do the best I can to relieve them. While I was preparing the food for the sick child, I heard the oldest boy (who was about fourteen), say: "You shall have the biggest piece now, because I had the biggest piece before." I turned around to see who it was that manifested such a principle of justice, and I saw four or five children sitting in the corner, where the oldest was dividing a roasted potato among them. And he said to one: "You shall have the biggest piece now," etc. But the other said: "Why, brother, you are the oldest, and you ought to have the biggest piece."

"No," said the other, "I had the biggest piece."

I turned to the mother, and said: "Madam, you have potatoes to eat, I suppose?"

She replied, "We have had, but this is the last one we have left; and the children have now roasted that for their breakfast."

On hearing this, I hastened home, and informed my wife that I had taken the wrong medicine with me to the sick family. I then prescribed a gallon of milk, two loaves of bread, some butter, meat and potatoes, and sent my boy with these; and had the pleasure to hear in a few days that they were all well. —*Selected.*

Only One Vote

A local option contest was going on in W——, and Mrs. Kent was trying to influence her husband to vote "No License." Willie Kent, six years old, was, of course on his mama's side. The night before election Mr. Kent went to see Willie safe in bed, and hushing his prattle, he said: "Now, Willie, say your prayers."

"Papa, I want to say my own words to-night," he replied. "All right, my boy, that is the best kind of praying," answered the father.

Fair was the picture, as Willie, robed in white, knelt at his father's knee and prayed reverently: "O dear Jesus, do help papa to vote No Whiskey tomorrow. Amen."

Morning came, the village was alive with excitement. Women's hands, made hard by toil, were stretched to God for help in the decision.

The day grew late and yet Mr. Kent had not been to the polls. Willie's prayer sounded in his ears, and troubled conscience said: "Answer your boy's petition with your ballot."

At last he stood at the polling-place with two tickets in his hand — one, license; the other, "No License." Sophistry, policy, avarice said: "Vote License." Conscience echoed: "No License." After a moment's hesitation, he threw from him the No License ticket and put the License in the box.

The next day it was found that the contest was so close that it needed but one vote to carry the town for prohibition. In the afternoon, Willie found a No Li-

cense ticket, and, having heard only one vote was nec-
essary, he started out to find the man who would cast
this one ballot against wrong, and in his eagerness he
flew along the streets.

The saloon men were having a jubilee, and the high-
ways were filled with drunken rowdies. Little Willie
rushed on through the unsafe crowd.

Hark! a random pistol-shot from a drunken quarrel, a
pierced heart, and sweet Willie Kent had his death-wound.

They carried him home to his mother. His father was
summoned, and the first swift thought that came to
him, as he stood over the lifeless boy, was: "Willie will

never pray again that I vote No Whiskey."

With a strange, still grief he took in his own the quiet
little hand chilling into marble coldness, and there between the fingers, firmly clasped, was the No License
ballot with which the brave little soul thought to change
the verdict of yesterday.

Mr. Kent started back in shame and sorrow. That
vote in his hand might have answered the prayer so
lately on his lips, now dumb, and perhaps averted the
awful calamity. Fathers, may not the hands of the
"thousands slain" make mute appeal to you? Your

one vote is what God requires of you. You are as re-
sponsible for it being in harmony with His law as if
on it hung the great decision. — *The Issue*.

How a Little Girl Utilized the Telephone.

A mother living not very far from the post-office in this
city, tired with watching over a sick baby, came down
stairs for a moment the other day for a few seconds rest.
She heard the voice of her little four-year-old girl in the
hall by herself, and, curious to know to whom she was
talking, stopped for a moment at the half-opened door.
She saw that the little thing had pulled a chair in front of
the telephone, and stood upon it, with the piece against

the side of her head. The earnestness of the child showed
that she was in no playing mood, and this was the conversation the mother heard, while the tears stood thick in
her eyes; the little one carrying on both sides, as if she
were repeating the answers:

"Hello."

"Well, who's there?"

"Is God there?"

"Yes."

"Is Jesus there?"

"Yes."

"Tell Jesus I want to speak to him."

"Well?"

"Is that you, Jesus?"

"Yes. What is it?"

"Our baby is sick, and we want you to let it get well. Won't you, now?"

No answer, and statement and question again repeated, and finally answered by a "Yes."

The little one put the ear-piece back on its hook, clambered down from the chair, and with a radiant face, went for her mother, who caught her in her arms.

The baby whose life had been despaired of, began to mend that day and got well. —*Elmira Free Press.*

The Dying Child's Prayer for Her Drunken Father.

A child from a poor family had an intemperate father, who often used to abuse his wife and children. This child had been to the Sunday-school—had become pious. The physician told the father that his little girl would die. No! he did not believe it. Yes, she will—she must die in a few hours. The father flew to the bedside; would not part with her, he said.

"Yes, father, you must part with me, I am going to Jesus. Promise me two things. One is, that you won't abuse mother any more, and will drink no more whiskey."

He promised in a solemn, steady manner. The little girl's face lighted up with joy.

"The other thing is, promise me that you will *pray*," said the child.

"I cannot pray; don't know how," said the poor

man. "Father, kneel down, please. There, take the words after me, I will pray; I learned how to pray in Sunday-school, and God has taught me how to pray too, my heart prays, and you must let your heart pray.

Now say the words."

And she began in her simple language to pray to the Savior of sinners. After a little he began to repeat after her; as he went on his heart was interested, and he broke out into an earnest prayer for himself; bewailed his sins, confessed and promised to forsake them; entered into covenant with God; light broke out of darkness; how long he prayed he did not know; he seemed to have forgotten his child in his prayer. When he came to himself he raised his head from the bed on which he had rested it; there lay the little speaker, a lovely smile was upon the face, her little hand was in that of the father, but she had gone to be among the angels. — *Power of Prayer by Prime.*

Lost Treasures.

"Come, Mamie, darling," said Mrs. Peterson, "before you go into the land of dreams you will kneel at my knee and thank your heavenly Father for what he has given you to-day."

Mamie came slowly towards her mother, and said, "I've been very naughty, and I can't pray, mamma. "

"If you've been naughty, dear, that is the more reason that you need to pray. ' '

"But, mamma, I don't think God wants little girls to come to Him when they are naughty."

"You are not naughty now, my dear, are you?"

"No, I am not naughty now."

"Well, then, come at once."

"What shall I say to God about it, mamma?"

"You can tell God how very sorry you are."

"What difference will that make?"

"When we have told God that we are sorry, and when he has forgiven us, then we are as happy as if we had not done wrong; but we cannot undo the mischief."

"Then, mamma, I can never be quite as rich as if I had not had a naughty hour today."

"Never, my dear; but the thought of your loss may help you to be more careful in the future, and we will ask God to keep you from sinning against him again." — *Selected.*

The Little Swiss Girl, Who Died to Save Her Father's Life

My dear little friend: I want to tell you about a little girl in Switzerland who died to save her father's life. I hope it will lead you to think of Him who died a dreadful death on the cross, that we might be saved from sin and sorrow here, and at last dwell with Him in bright mansions in the skies.

This little girl lived near a deep ravine at the foot of one of the mountains in Switzerland. A huge rock had fallen down the mountain side, and lodged in the ravine, and thus made a natural bridge, so that those who wished to pass from one side of the mountain to the other, could cross the bridge. The mother of the child was an earnest Christian, and often told her daughter about the blessed Savior, who died in the place of sinners, who deserved to be punished, that they might be forgiven and saved in heaven. And she told her also that unless she came to Jesus, and trusted in Him, she would be lost forever. At first the little girl did not care very much about what her mother said, but at last the mother's prayer was answered. Her little one felt herself to be a lost sinner, and that Christ alone could save her. God's spirit taught her that Jesus had paid the debt, and that He stood with open arms ready to receive her, and wash her sins away. Then she felt sure that heaven would be her home forever. Her father was not a Christian. He never gathered his loved ones around the family altar.

One day when about to cross the deep ravine upon the rock bridge, the mother saw that it was just ready to fall. The frost had loosened it. She told her little child that if she ever crossed it again it would fall, and she would be dashed in pieces.

The next day the father told his child that he was going over to the other side across the bridge. She said to him it was not safe, but he only laughed at her. He said he had been across it before she was born, and that he was not afraid. When the dear little thing saw that he was determined to go, she asked if she could go with him.

While they were walking along together, she looked up into her father's face, and said: "Father, if I should die, will you promise to love Jesus and meet me in heaven?"

"Pshaw!" he said, "what put such a wild thought into your head? You are not going to die, I hope. You are only a wee thing, and will live many years."

"Yes, but if I should die, will you promise to love Jesus just as I do, and meet me in heaven?"

"But you are not going to die. Don't speak of it," he said.

"But if I should die, do promise, Father, you will be a good Christian and come up and live with Jesus and me in heaven."

"Yes, yes!" he said at last.

When they came near the crossing-place, she said: "father, please stand here a minute." She loved him dearly and was willing to run the risk of dying for him. Strange as it may seem, she walked quickly and jumped upon the loose rock, and down it went with the girl. She was crushed to death. The trembling parent crept to the edge, and eyes dimmed with tears, gazed wildly upon the wreck. Then he thought of all his little child had told him about how Jesus had died to save us. He thought he had never loved her so much. But he began to see that he had far more reason to love Jesus who had suffered much more to save him from the "bottomless pit." And then he thought of the promise he so carefully made to his daughter. What could he do but kneel down and cry to God to have mercy upon him?

If they meet in heaven, do you think that daughter will be sorry that she sacrificed her life for her father's sake? Can you not imagine that tears often filled the eyes of that father when he spoke of his sainted little one?

You would say that he would have been a very wicked man if he had not loved the memory of his child. But is it not a thousand times more wicked for you not to love Him who has loved you so much more than that little one loved her father?

How can you help loving such a precious Savior? Will you not ask Him to forgive you and help you to live for Him the rest of your life? — *The Way of Faith.*

"Forgotten My Soul"

"Mother, you have forgotten my soul," so said a little girl, three years old, as her kind and careful mother was about to lay her in bed. She had just risen from repeating the Lord's prayer. "But, mother," she said, "you have forgotten my soul."

"What do you mean, Anna?"

"Why,

"Now I lay me down to sleep,
I pray the Lord my soul to keep;
If I should die before I wake,
I pray the Lord my soul to take."

We have not said that."

The child meant nothing more, yet her words were startling. And, oh! from how many rosy lips might they come with mournful significance!" You, fond mother, so busy hour after hour preparing and adorning garments for their pretty little form, have you forgotten the soul? Do you commend it earnestly to the care of its God and Savior? Are you leading it to commit itself, in faith and love, to his keeping? — *Selected*.

Prevailing Prayer of a Child

At the close of a prayer-meeting, the pastor observed a little girl about twelve years of age remaining upon her

knees, when most of the congregation had retired. Thinking the child had fallen asleep, he touched her and told her it was time to return home. To his surprise he found that she was engaged in prayer, and he said: "All things whatsoever ye shall ask in prayer, believing, ye shall receive." She looked up at the pastor earnestly, and inquired: "Is that so? Does God say that?" He took up a Bible and read the passage aloud. She immediately began praying: "Lord, send my father here; Lord, send my father to the church." Thus she continued for about half an hour, attracting by her earnest cry the attentions of persons who had lingered about the door. At last a man rushed into the church, ran up the aisle and sank upon his knees by the side of his child, exclaiming: "What do you want of me?" She threw her arms about his neck, and began to pray: "Oh, Lord, convert my father!" Soon the man's heart was melted and he began to pray for himself. The child's father was three miles from the church when she began praying for him. He was packing goods in a wagon and felt impressed with an irresistible impulse to return home. Driving rapidly to his house, he left the goods in his wagon and hastened to the church, where he found his daughter crying mightily to God in his behalf; and he was led there to the Savior.— *Foster's Cyclopædia*.

The Dying News Boy.

In a dark alley in the great city of New York, a small, ragged boy might be seen. He appeared to be about twelve years old, and had a careworn expression on his countenance. The cold air seemed to have no pity as it pierced through his ragged clothes, and made the flesh beneath blue and almost frozen.

This poor boy had once a happy home. His parents died a year before, and left him without money or friends. He was compelled to face the cold, cruel world with but a few cents in his pocket. He tried to earn his living by selling newspapers and other such things. This day everything seemed to go against him, and in despair he threw himself down in the dark alley, with his papers by his side. A few boys gathered around the poor lad, and asked in a kind way (for a street Arab): "Say, Johnny, why don't you go to the lodges?" (The lodge was a place where almost all the boys stayed at night, costing but a few cents.) But the poor little lad could only murmur that he could not stir, and called the boys about him, saying: "I am dying now, because I feel so queer; and I can hardly see you. Gather around me closer, boys. I cannot talk so loud. I can kinder see the angels holding out their hands for me to come to that beautiful place called heaven. Good-bye, boys. I am to meet father and mother." And, with these last words on his lips, the poor lad died.

"I am dying now, because I feel so queer; and I can hardly see you. I can kinder see the angels holding out their hands for me to come to that beautiful place they call heaven."

Next morning the passers-by saw a sight that would soften the most hardened heart. There, lying on the cold stone, with his head against the hard wall, and his eyes staring upward, was the poor little frozen newsboy. He was taken to the church near by, and was interred by kind hands. And those who performed this act will never forget the poor forsaken lad. — *Golden Dawn.*

New Shoes.

"I wonder if there can be a pair of shoes in it!"

Little Tim sat on the ground close beside a very ugly dark-colored stone jug. He eyed it sharply, but finding it quite impossible to see through its sides, pulled out the cork and peered anxiously in. "Can't see nothin', but its [sic] so dark in there I couldn't see if there was anything. I've a great mind to break the hateful old thing."

He sat for awhile thinking how badly he wanted a pair of shoes to wear to the Sunday-school picnic. His mother had promised to wash and mend his clothes, so that he might go looking very neat indeed; but the old shoes were far past all mending and how could he go barefoot?

Then he began counting the chances of his father being very angry when he should find his jug broken. He did not like the idea of getting a whipping for it, as was very likely, but how could he resist the temptation of making sure about those shoes? The more he thought of them, the more he couldn't. He sprang up and hunted around until he found a good size brick-bat, which he flung with such vigorous hand and correct aim that the next moment the old jug lay in pieces before his eyes.

How eagerly he bent over them in the hope of finding not only what he was so longing for but, perhaps, other treasure! But his poor little heart sank as he turned over the fragments with trembling fingers. Nothing could be found among the broken bits, wet on the inside with a bad-smelling liquid.

Tim sat down again and sobbed as he had never sobbed before; so hard that he did not hear a step beside him until a voice said:

"Well! what's all this?"

He sprang up in great alarm. It was his father, who always slept late in the morning, and was very seldom awake so early as this.

"Who broke my jug?" he asked. "I did," said Tim, catching his breath half in terror and half between his sobs.

"Why did you?" Tim looked up. The voice did not sound quite so terrible as he had expected. The truth was his father had been touched at sight of the forlorn figure, so very small and so sorrowful, which had bent over the broken jug.

"Why," he said, "I was lookin' for a pair of new shoes. I want a pair of shoes awful bad to wear at the picnic. All the other chaps wear shoes."

"How came you to think you'd find shoes in a jug?"

"Why, mamma said so. I asked her for some new shoes, and she said they had gone into the black jug, and that lots of other things had gone into it, too—coats and hats, and bread and meat and things—and I thought if I broke it I'd find 'em all, and there ain't a thing in it—and

mamma never said what wasn't so before—and I thought
't would be so—sure."

And Tim, hardly able to sob out the words, feeling
how keenly his trust in mother's word had added to
his great disappointment, sat down again, and cried
harder than ever.

His father seated himself on a box in the disorderly
yard, and remained quiet for so long a time that Tim at
last looked timidly up.

"I am real sorry I broke your jug, Father. I'll never do
it again."

"No, I guess you won't," he said, laying a hand on the
rough little head as he went away, leaving Tim overcome
with astonishment that his father had not been angry
with him.

Two days after, on the very evening before the picnic,
he handed Tim a parcel, telling him to open it.

"New shoes! new shoes!" he shouted. "Oh, father, did
you get a new jug and were they in it?"

"No, my boy, there isn't going to be a new jug. Your
mother was right all the time—the things all went into
the jug; but you see getting them out is no easy matter so I am going to keep them out after this." —*New
York Observer*

Little Jennie's Sickness and Death
BY HER MOTHER

Little Jennie was eight years old, March 30, 1886. The
April following she was taken very sick, and from that
time until June 4, she seemed a little suffering angel. Then
Jesus, who had so blessedly sustained her during all her
sufferings, took her to Himself. She would say, when able
to talk: "Mamma, I do not care what I suffer, God knows
best." When she was very low, we would often see her
dear lips moving, and listening, hear her praying. She
would finish her prayer and after saying "Amen," hav-

ing noticed that we were listening to her, would look up into our faces to see if we wanted anything. This patience and devotion characterized her whole life. Often, when she was at play with her sister, who was the older by five years, when some little trouble would arise, she would take her sister by the hand and say: "Kittie, let's tell Jesus." Then bowing her little head, she would pour out her whole heart in prayer to God, with the fervency that is shown by a true Christian.

About three weeks after she was taken ill, her little body was paralyzed and drawn all out of shape it seemed. Then in a few days her little limbs were so we could almost straighten them. What suffering she endured all that time, no one knows but those who were with her.

May 25th, which was Tuesday, while suffering terribly, she said: "Mamma, play and sing." I took my guitar, and without stopping to think what to sing, began that beautiful song in the Gospel Hymns: "Nearer my home, to-day, than I have been before." I could praise God just then, for I was filled with His Spirit. She lay there looking at me with her little blue eyes and trying in her weak voice to help me. At last she seemed soothed by the music. But we knew that Jesus, in His infinite love, had quieted her for a time, because we were willing to submit to His will. We had said all the time: "Lord, not my will, but thine."

She rested quite well until about three o'clock in the afternoon; then suddenly she spoke and her voice sounded quite strong. She said: "Oh, mamma, see those people, how funny they look! They look like poles." She was lying so that she could look out of the window, and as she spoke her eyes seemed to rest on some object there. Then she spoke louder; "*Oh, mamma, come and see the little children!* I never saw so many in my life." I sat down on the front of the bed and said: "Jennie, is there any there that you know?" She looked them over so earnestly, then said: "No, not one." I asked her how they looked. She said: "Mamma, every one has a gold crown on its head, and they are all dressed in white." I thought that Jesus was coming for her then. After telling me that there were none that she knew she sank back on the pillows exhausted. But in a few moments she raised up again and said: "Oh, mamma, hear that music! Did you ever hear such grand music? Now, do not shut the windows to-night, will you?" I told her that I would not.

The next morning she called Kittie into the room and said: "Kittie, I want to tell you what I saw last night." She then proceeded to tell her the same as she had told me the evening before. Then she said: "Now, Kittie, you will forgive me for ever being cross to you won't you?" Kittie answered, "Little darling, you have never been cross to me. Will you forgive me, sister, for being cross to you?" "Darling sister," she said, "that is all right."

Thursday night she was paralyzed in her left side, so that she had no use of it. Friday all day she lay unconscious, and that night the same. Saturday, about ten o'clock, she commenced to try and whisper. We could hear her say: "Papa, mamma." We tried to understand her, but at first could not. She kept whispering plainer, and finally we heard her say: "Take—me—up—stairs. I—want—to—lie—on—my—own—bed—once—more." But of course we could not move her. Suddenly she said aloud: "I am going to die! kiss me quick, mamma." I bent down and kissed her, and she looked so wretched. I said: "Jennie, you will not have to go alone; Jesus will take you." She answered: "I know it. I wish that He would come this minute. Kiss me again, mamma." I did so; then she wished us to sing. Again, without giving one thought, I commenced singing the same words that I sang the Tuesday before. She raised her right hand arm's length, and began to wave it and bow her head. Oh! she was so happy.

"They brought the guitar, and she continued to wave her little hand, while I played and sang the whole piece."

Then she said: "Play." They brought the guitar, and she continued to wave her little hand, while I played and sang the whole piece. One of her aunts, standing near the bed took hold of her hand to stop it, but it moved just the same; and I said: "Ollie, let go of her hand, that is the Lord's doings." After I finished, she kissed her father, mother and sister and bade them good-bye; then called four other very dear friends and told them good-bye after kissing them. She then called for a book and wanted the music teacher, who was present, to play and sing a piece which she dearly loved.

Before she was sick she would have little prayer-meetings, and her sweet little face would shine with happiness. She would say: "Oh, mamma, how the Lord has blessed me."

While the dear teacher was playing and singing her favorite, she was waving her little hand. We sang three or four other pieces around her bed. We all thought that Jesus would take her then. Oh, what joy; it was heaven below. Jesus was there and the room was filled with glory on account of His presence. Two of her aunts said that it seemed as though they were in heaven.

She never spoke after that, but would try to make us understand by motioning when she wanted anything. Sometimes it would take us a long time, but she would be so patient. She was ready and waiting. She had peace that the world cannot give, and, praise God! that the world cannot take away. The dear little one lived until the next Tuesday afternoon, and went to Jesus about three o'clock. That was the time she saw the vision the Tuesday before. Tuesday morning before daylight she tried to tell me something. I said: "Sing?" She looked so happy and bowed her head. I began singing: "I am Jesus' little lamb." She bowed her head again. In the forenoon she kept looking at her aunts, Ollie and Belle, and pointing up. Oh! it meant so much. It seemed to me that she was saying, that it meant: "Meet me in heaven." Finally she motioned for me to raise the window-curtain. I did so and she looked out the window so eagerly, as though she was expecting to see the little children. Then the little blue eyes closed to open no more in this world, but in heaven. — *Mrs. Libbie Jones.*

She Died for Him.

A poor emigrant had gone to Australia to "make his fortune," leaving a wife and little son in England. When he had made some money, he wrote home to his wife:

"Come out to me here; I send the money for your passage; I want to see you and my boy." The wife took ship as soon as she could, and started for her new home. One night, as they were all asleep there sounded the dreaded cry of "Fire, fire!" Everyone rushed on deck and the boats were soon filled. The last one was just pushing off, when a cry of "there are two more on deck," arose. They were the mother and her son. Alas! "Only room for one," the sailors shouted. Which was to go? The mother thought of her far-away home, her husband looking out lovingly and longingly for his wife. Then she glanced at the boy, clinging frightened to her skirts. She could not let him die. There was no time to lose. Quick! quick! the flames were getting around. Snatching the child she held him to her a moment. "Willie, tell father I died for you!" Then the boy was lowered into the sailors' willing arms. She died for him. — *Selected*.

"I Don't Love You Now, Mother."

A great many years ago I knew a lady who had been sick for two years, as you have seen many a one, all the while slowly dying with consumption. She had one child — a little boy named Henry.

One afternoon I was sitting by her side, and it seemed as if she would cough her life away. Her little boy stood by the post of the bed, his blue eyes filled with tears to see her suffer so. By and by the terrible cough ceased. Henry came and put his arms around his mother's neck, nestled his head in his mother's bosom, and said, "Mother, I do love you; I wish you wasn't sick."

An hour later, the same loving, blue-eyed boy came in all aglow, stamping the snow off his feet.

"O, Mother, may I go a-skating? it is so nice — Ed and Charlie are going." "Henry," feebly said the mother, "the ice is not hard enough yet." "But, Mother," very pettishly said the boy, "you are sick all the time — how do you know?" "My child, you must obey me," gently said his mother.

"It is too bad," angrily sobbed the boy, who an hour ago, had so loved his mother. "I would not like to have my little boy go," said his mother, looking sadly at the little boy's face, all covered with frowns; "you said you loved me—be good." "No, I don't love you now, mother," said the boy, going out and slamming the door.

Again that dreadful coughing came upon her, and *we* thought no more of the boy. After the coughing had commenced, I noticed tears falling thick upon her pillow, but she sank from exhaustion into a light sleep.

In a little while muffled steps of men's feet were heard coming into the house, as though carrying something; and they were carrying the almost lifeless body of Henry.

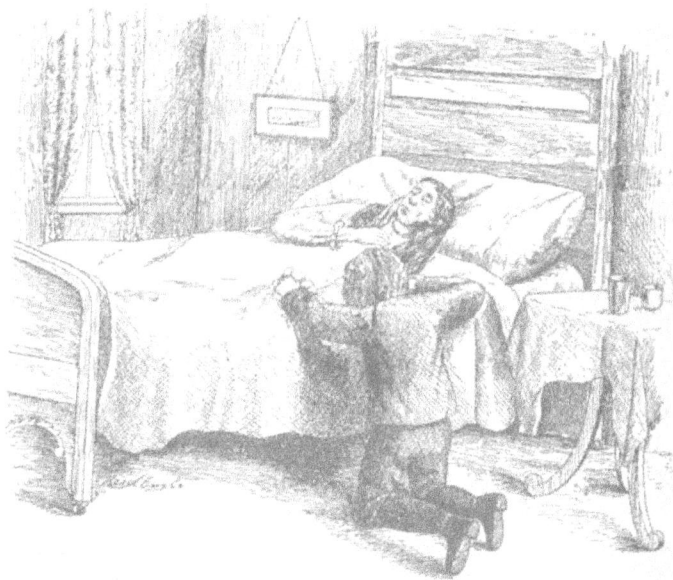

Angrily had he left his mother and gone to skate—disobeying her; and then broken through the ice, sunk under the water, and now saved by a great effort, was brought home barely alive to his sick mother.

I closed the doors feeling more danger for her life than the child's, and coming softly in, drew back the curtains from the bed. She spoke, "I heard them—it is Henry; Oh, I knew he went—is he dead?" But she never seemed to hear the answer I gave her. She commenced coughing—she died in agony—strangled to death. The poor mother! The boy's disobedience killed her.

After a couple of hours I sought the boy's room. "Oh, I wish I had not told mother I did not love her. To-morrow I will tell her I do," said the child sobbing painfully. My heart ached; to-morrow I knew we must tell him she was dead. We did not till the child came fully into the room, crying, "Mother, I do love you." Oh! may I never see agony like that child's, as the lips he kissed gave back no kiss, as the hands he took fell lifeless from his hand, instead of shaking his hand as it always had, and the boy knew she was dead.

"Mother, I do love you now," all the day he sobbed and cried, "O mother, mother, forgive me." Then he would not leave his mother. "Speak to me, mother!" but she could never speak again, and he—the last words she had ever heard him say, were, "Mother, I don't love you now."

That boy's whole life was changed; sober and sad he was ever after. He is now a gray haired old man, with one sorrow over his one act of disobedience, one wrong word embittering all his life— with those words ever ringing in his ears, "Mother, I don't love you now."

Will the little ones who read this remember, if they disobey their mother, if they are cross and naughty, they say every single time they do so, to a tender mother's heart, by their actions if not in the words of Henry, the very same thing, "I don't love you now, mother."

"Little Mother."

She was a clear-eyed, fresh-cheeked little maiden, living on the banks of the great Mississippi, the oldest of four children, and mother's "little woman" always. They called her so because of her quiet, matronly care of the younger Mayfields—that was the father's name. Her own name was the beautiful one of Elizabeth, but they shortened it to Bess.

She was thirteen when one day Mr. Mayfield and his wife were called to the nearest town, six miles away. "Be mother's little woman, dear," said Mrs. Mayfield, as she kissed the rosy face. Her husband added: "I leave the children in your care, Bess: be a little mother to them."

Bess waved her old sun-bonnet vigorously, and held up the baby Rose, that she might watch them to the last. Old Daddy Jim and Mammy had been detailed by Mr. Mayfield to keep an unsuspected watch on the little nestlings, and were to sleep at the house. Thus two days went by, when Daddy Jim and Mammy begged to be allowed to go to the quarters where the negroes lived, to see their daughter "Jinnie, who was pow'ful bad wid the toothache." They declared they would be back by evening, so Bess was willing. She put the little girls to bed and persuaded Rob to go; then seated herself by the table with her mother's work-basket, in quaint imitation of Mrs. Mayfield's industry in the evening time. But what was this? Her feet touched something cold! She bent down and felt around with her hand. A pool of water was spreading over the floor. She knew what it was; the Mississippi had broken through the levee. What should she do? Mammy's stories of how houses had been washed away and broken in pieces, were in her mind. "Oh, if I had a boat!" she exclaimed, "but there isn't anything of the sort on the place." She ran wildly out to look for Mammy; and stumbled over something sitting near the edge of the porch. A sudden inspiration took her. Here was her boat! a very large, old-fashioned, oblong tub. The water was now several inches deep on the porch and she contrived to half-float, half-row the tub into the room.

Without frightening the children she got them dressed in the warmest clothes they had. She lined the oblong tub with a blanket, and made ready bread and cold meat left from supper. With Rob's assistance she dragged the tub upstairs. There was a single large window in the room, and they set the tub directly by it, so that when the water rose the tub would float out. There was no way for the children to reach the roof, which was a very steep, inclined one. It did not seem long before the water had very nearly risen to the top of the stairs leading from below.

Bess flung the window open, and made Rob get into their novel boat; then she lifted in Kate, and finally baby Rose, who began to cry, was given into Rob's arms, and

now the little mother, taking the basket of food, made ready to enter, too; but, lo! there was no room for her with safety to the rest. Bess paused a moment, drew a long breath, and kissed the children quietly. She explained to Rob that he must guard the basket, and that they must sit still. "Good-bye, dears. Say a prayer for sister, Rob. If you ever see father and mother, tell them I took care of you." Then the water seized the insecure vessel, and out into the dark night it floated.

The next day Mr. Mayfield, who, with his neighbors, scoured the broad lake of eddying water that represented the Mississippi, discovered the tub lodged in the branches of a sycamore with the children weeping and chilled, but safe.

And Bess? Ah, where was Bess, the "little mother," who in that brief moment resigned herself to death? They found her later, floating on the water with her brave childish face turned to the sky; and as strong arms lifted her into the boat, the tears from every eye paid worthy tribute to the "little mother." — *Detroit Free Press.*

Robbie Goodman's Prayer.

[Christians of different denominations, and even members of the same denomination, too, often allow their differences of opinion to result in prejudice and lack of brotherly love. We commend to all the lesson taught by the following incident. — ED.]

"What can be the matter with Walter," thought Mamma Ellis as she sat sewing in her pleasant sitting-room. "He came in so very quietly, closed the door gently and I think I even heard him go to the closet to hang up his books. Oh! dear. I hope he isn't going to have another attack of 'Grippe,'" and Mrs. Ellis shivered as she glanced out at the snow-covered landscape. As her eyes turned once more to the warm, luxurious room in which she was seated, the portiers were pushed aside and a little boy of ten years of age entered. Little Walter was all that remained of four beautiful children, who, only a year ago, romped gaily through the large halls. That dread disease, diphtheria, had stolen the older brother and laughing little sisters in one short week's time, so that now, as the sad anniversary came near to hand, Mrs. Ellis' heart ached for her lost birdlings and yearned more jealously than ever over her remaining little one. To-day his usually merry face was very grave and he looked very thoughtful as he gave his mother her kiss and allowed himself to be drawn upon her lap. "What ails mother's pet? Is he sick?" she asked anxiously. "No, mother dear, I'm not sick, but I feel so sad at heart. You see," he continued in answer to her questioning look, "Robbie Goodman and I always walk together going and coming from school, and I have noticed that he has never worn any overcoat this winter, but you know its been unusually warm and I thought perhaps his mother did not make him wrap up like you did me, but this morning it was so cold and he was just shivering, but he never had on any overcoat. Just his mittens and muffler and cap were his wraps. Of course I noticed it for nearly everyone else was all bundled up, but I didn't say anything as I did not want to be im-

polite. After awhile he said, 'My, I am so cold,' and I said: 'Where's your overcoat?' Then he told me it was too small and his papa can't buy him any this winter so he is afraid he will have to stop school. His mamma says she would cut his papa's up for him, only then he would not have any; and of course he must have one to wear when he goes to church and to see sick people. Even that one is thin and patched. He says he and his little sisters have been praying so hard for an over-coat for him and shoes for them but they did not come at Christmas like they thought they would, and they are real discouraged. To-night, mother," continued Walter, "he had an awful cold and coughed just like our Harry did last year," and the long pent up tears flowed from the child's eyes. As mother and son dried their tears, the child looked up with perfect confidence as he said, "The Lord will answer Robbie's prayer, won't he, mamma?" "Yes darling," said Mrs. Ellis, and sent the child off to the play-room.

"By-the-way, my dear," remarked Mrs. Ellis as they sat chatting at the tea-table after Walter had retired, "what has become of that preacher Goodman who preached for us once on trial?" "Oh, he has a mission down on the other side of the city, but he lives on this side as Moore gives him the house rent free. I met him the other day. He looked very seedy. The man had wonderful talents and might have a rich church and improve himself, but he is persistent in his ideas concerning this holiness movement, and of course a large church like ours wants something to attract and interest instead of such egotistical discourses. I, for one, go to sleep under them." And Mr. Ellis drew himself up with a pompous air as he went into the library, whither his wife presently followed. He had picked up a newspaper and was apparently absorbed, but Mrs. Ellis had not had her say, so she continued: "Walter was telling me about the little boy. He—" "Oh, yes," interrupted her husband, "he met me in the hall and poured out the whole story. The child's nerves were all wrought up, too. He should not be allowed to worry over such things. He wants me to give up buying him the fur-trimmed overcoat and get a coat and shoes for Goodman's children, as they were praying so hard for them, but I have enough to do without clothing other people's children. If Goodman would quit his cranky notions and use his talents for people who could understand him, instead of preaching to those ragamuffins he might now be receiving a magnificent salary and clothing himself and family decently." "But Paul," said Mrs. Ellis, "surely you would not have Mr. Goodman sacrifice his convictions simply for money and praise, when you yourself, are convinced that his doctrines are sound? Besides he must be doing a good work down among the poor

classes of the city as it appears the rich don't want him." "Then let the poor give enough to keep him." "They do give far beyond their means but the Lord calls on such as us to give. I know it has been an unusually hard year but the Lord has blessed us and he will hold us to an account. I feel very sad as the anniversary of our darlings' departure draws near and I dread to think of any little ones suffering while we could so easily help them." "I don't see how you can feel that we have been so blessed. When the house is so quiet and I think of those white graves in the cemetery I confess I feel very bitter." "Paul, my dear husband, don't feel that way. Just think of our three treasures in heaven, an added claim to that glorious realm, away from this cold and suffering. Remember also that we have one left, to live for, to train. And, Paul, let us train him for the Master and in such a way that we may never have the feeling that it were better if he, too, had departed when he was pure and innocent. Let us encourage benevolence and gentleness and if he wishes to go without the fur-trimmed coat, why not do as he asks?" Mrs. Ellis kissed her husband and quietly left the room. Long and late, Paul Ellis sat there and many things, ghosts of the past, rose before him. As the midnight chimes rang out he knelt and prayed. "Oh, Lord, forgive me. I have gone astray and turned to my own way. I have been prejudiced. It was my influence which turned the tide against Robert Goodman. Thou knowest. Now, if thou wilt only forgive and help me I will walk in the light as thou sendest it even consenting to be called a 'holiness crank.'"

A few days afterward Robert Goodman received a large package from an unknown friend containing a warm overcoat and three pairs of shoes. His father also received a present. It came through the mail and was an honest confession of a wrong done him, also a check for one hundred dollars. One year later First church gave a unanimous call to Rev. Goodman and the revival which broke out that winter was unprecedented in the annals of that church. Verily, "A little child shall lead them." —*Luella Watson Kinder, in Christian Witness.*

Carletta and the Merchant.

"If I could only have your faith, gladly would I—but I was born a skeptic. I cannot look upon God and the future as *you* do."

So said John Harvey as he walked with a friend under a dripping umbrella. John Harvey was a skeptic of thirty years standing and apparently hardened in his unbelief. Everybody had given him up as hopeless. Reasoning ever so calmly made no impression on the rocky soil of his heart. Alas! it was sad, very sad!

But one friend had never given him up. When spoken to about him—"I will talk with and pray for that man until I die," he said; "and I will have faith that he may yet come out of darkness into the marvelous light."

And thus whenever he met him (John Harvey was always ready for a "talk,") Mr. Hawkins pressed home the truth. In answer, on that stormy night, he said: "God can change a skeptic, John. He has more power over your heart than you, and I mean still to pray for you."

"Oh, I have no objections, none in the world—seeing is believing, you know. I'm ready for any miracle; but I tell you it would take nothing short of a miracle to convince me. Let's change the subject. I'm hungry and it's too far to go up town to supper on this stormy night. Here's a restaurant; let us stop here."

How warm and pleasant it looked in the long, brilliant dining saloon!

The two merchants had eaten, and were just on the point of rising when a strain of soft music came through the open door—a child's sweet voice.

" 'Pon my word, that is pretty," said John Harvey; "what purity in those tones!"

"Out of here, you little baggage!" cried a hoarse voice, and one of the waiters pointed angrily to the door.

"Let her come in," said John Harvey.

"We don't allow them in this place, sir," said the waiter, "but she can go into the reading-room."

"Well, let her go somewhere. I want to hear her," responded the gentleman.

All this time the two had seen the shadow of something hovering backwards and forwards on the edge of the door; now they followed a slight little figure, wrapped in a patched cloak, patched hood, and leaving the mark of wet feet as she walked. Curious to see her face—she was very small—John Harvey lured her to the farthest part of the great room where there were but few gentlemen, and then motioned her to sing. The little one looked timidly up. Her cheek was of olive darkness, but a flush rested there, and out of the thinnest face, under the arch of broad temples, deepened by masses of the blackest hair looked two eyes whose softness and tender pleading would have touched the hardest heart.

"That little thing is sick, I believe," said John Harvey, compassionately. "What do you sing, child?" he added.

"I sing Italian or a little English."

John Harvey looked at her shoes. "Why," he exclaimed, and his lips quivered, "her feet are wet to her ankles; she will catch her death of cold."

By this time the child had begun to sing, pushing back her hood, and folding before her her little thin fingers. Her voice was wonderful; and simple and common as were both air and words, the pathos of the tones drew together several of the merchants in the reading-room. The little song commenced thus:

"There is a happy land,
   Far, far away."

Never could the voice, the manner, of that child be forgotten. There almost seemed a halo around her head; and when she had finished, her great speaking eyes turned toward John Harvey.

"Look here, child; where did you learn that song?" he asked.

"At the Sabbath-school, Sir."

"And you don't suppose there *is* a happy land?" he continued, heedless of the many eyes upon him.

"I know there is; I'm going to sing there," she said, so quietly, so decidedly, that the men looked at each other.

"Going to sing there?"

"Yes, sir. My mother said so. She used to sing to me until she was very sick. Then she said she wasn't going to sing any more on earth, but up in heaven."

"Well—and what then?"

"And then she died, sir," said the child; tears brimming down the dark cheek, now ominously flushed scarlet.

John Harvey was silent for a few moments. Presently he said: "Well, if she died, my little girl, you may live, you know."

"Oh, no, sir! no, sir! I'd rather go there; and be with mother. Sometimes I have a dreadful pain in my side and cough as she did. There won't be any pain up there, sir; it's a beautiful world!"

"How do you know?" faltered on the lips of the skeptic.

"My mother told me so, sir."

Words how impressive! manner how child-like, and yet so wise!

John Harvey had had a praying mother. His chest labored for a moment—the sobs that struggled for utterance could be heard even in their depths—and still those large, soft, lustrous eyes, like magnets impelled his glance toward them.

"Child, you must have a pair of shoes."

John Harvey's voice was husky.

Hands were thrust in pockets, purses pulled out, and the astonished child held in her little palm more money than she had ever seen before.

"Her father is a poor, consumptive organ-grinder," whispered one. "I suppose he's too sick to be out to-night."

Along the soggy street went the child, under the protection of John Harvey, but not with shoes that drank the water at every step. Warmth and comfort were her's [sic] now. Down in the deep den-like lanes of the city walked the man, a little cold hand in his. At an open door they stopped; up broken, creaking stairs they climbed. Another doorway was opened, and a wheezing voice called out of the dim arch, "Carletta!"

"O father! father! see what I have brought you! look at me! look at me!" and down went the silver, and venting her joy, the poor child fell; crying and laughing together, into the old man's arms.

Was he a man?

A face dark and hollow, all overgrown with hair black as night and uncombed—a pair of wild eyes—a body bent nearly double— hands like claws.

"Did he give you all this, my child?"

"They all did, Father; now you shall have soup and oranges."

"Thank you, sir—I'm sick, you see—all gone, sir!—had to send the poor child out, or we'd starve. God bless you, sir! I wish I was well enough to play you a tune," and he looked wistfully towards the corner where stood the old organ, baize-covered, the baize in tatters.

One month after that the two men met again as if by agreement, and walked slowly down town. Treading innumerable passages they came to the gloomy building where lived Carletta's father.

No—not lived *there*; for as they paused a moment out came two or three men bearing a pine coffin. In the coffin slept the old organ-grinder.

"It was very sudden, sir," said a woman, who recognized his benefactor. "Yesterday the little girl was took sick, and it seemed as if he drooped right away. He died at six last night."

The two men went silently up stairs. The room was empty of everything save a bed, a chair and a nurse provided by John Harvey. The child lay there, not white, but pale as marble, with a strange polish on her brow.

"Well, my little one, are you better?"

"Oh, no, sir; father is gone up there and I am going."

Up *there!* John Harvey turned unconsciously towards his friend.

"Did you ever hear of Jesus?" asked John Harvey's friend.

"Oh yes."

"Do you know who he was?"

"*Good* Jesus," murmured the child.

"Hawkins, this breaks me down," said John Harvey and he placed his handkerchief to his eyes. "Don't cry, don't cry; *I* can't cry, I'm so glad," said the child exultingly.

"What are you glad for, my dear?" asked John Harvey's friend.

"To get away from here," she said deliberately. "I used to be so cold in the winter, for we didn't have fire sometimes; but mother used to hug me close and sing about heaven. Mother told me to never mind and kissed me and said if I was His, the Savior would love me and one

of these days would give me a better home, and so I gave myself to Him, for I wanted a better home. And, Oh, I shall sing there and be so happy!"

With a little sigh she closed her eyes.

"Harvey, are faith and hope nothing?" asked Mr. Hawkins.

"Don't speak to me, Hawkins; to be as that little child I would give all I have."

"And to be like her you need give nothing — only your stubborn will, your skeptical doubts, and the heart that will never know rest till at the feet of Christ."

There was no answer. Presently the hands moved, the arms were raised, the eyes opened — yet, glazed though they were they turned still upward.

"See!" she cried; ["]Oh, there is mother! and angels! and they are all singing."

Her voice faltered, but the celestial brightness lingered yet on her face.

"There is no doubting the soul-triumph there," whispered Mr. Hawkins.

"It is wonderful," replied John Harvey, looking on both with awe and tenderness. "Is she gone?"

He sprang from his chair as if he would detain her; but the chest and forehead were marble now, the eyes had lost the fire of life; she must have died as she lay looking at them.

"She was always a sweet little thing," said the nurse softly.

John Harvey stood as if spell-bound. There was a touch on his arm; he started.

"John," said his friend, with an affectionate look, "shall we pray?"

For a minute there was no answer—then came tears; the whole frame of the subdued skeptic shook as he said—it was almost a cry: "Yes, pray, pray!"

And from the side of the dead child went up agonizing pleadings to the throne of God. And that prayer was answered—the miracle was wrought—the lion became a lamb—the doubter a believer—the skeptic a Christian!—*A Tract.*

How Three Sunday School Children Met Their Fate.

When the Lawrence Mills were on fire a number of years ago—I don't mean on fire, but when the mill fell in—the great mill fell in, and after it had fallen in, the ruins caught fire. There was only one room left entire, and in it were three Mission Sunday- school children imprisoned. The neighbors and all hands got their shovels, and picks, and crowbars, and were working to set the children free. It came on night, and they had not yet reached the children. When they were near them, by some mischance the lantern broke, and the ruins caught fire. They tried to put it out, but could not succeed. They could talk with the children, and even pass to them some

The children saw their fate. They then knelt down and commenced to pray.

coffee and some refreshments, and encourage them to keep up. But, alas, the flames drew nearer and nearer to the prison. Superhuman were the efforts made to rescue the children; the men bravely fought back the flames; but the fire gained fresh strength, and returned to claim its victims. Then piercing shrieks arose when the spectators saw that the efforts of the firemen were hopeless. The children saw their fate. They then knelt down and commenced to sing the little hymn we have all been taught in our Sunday-school days, oh! how sweet: "Let others seek a home below, which flames devour and waves overflow." The flames had now reached them; the stifling smoke began to pour into their little room, and they began to sink, one by one, upon the floor. A few moments more and the fire circled around them, and their souls were taken into the bosom of Christ. Yes, let others seek a home below if they will, but seek ye the Kingdom of God with all your hearts.—*Moody's Anecdotes*

He Blesses God for the Faith of His Little Girl.

"I came home one night very late," says Rev. Matthew Hale Smith, in his *Marvels of Prayer*, "and had gone to bed to seek needed rest. The friend with whom I boarded awoke me out of my first refreshing sleep, and informed me that a little girl wanted to see me. I turned over in bed and said:

" 'I am very tired, tell her to come in the morning and I will see her.'

"My friend soon returned and said:

"'I think you had better get up. The girl is a poor little suffering thing. She is thinly clad, is without bonnet or shoes. She has seated herself on the doorstep and says she must see you and will wait till you get up.'

"I dressed myself and opening the outside door I saw one of the most forlorn looking little girls I ever beheld. Want, sorrow, suffering, neglect, seemed to struggle for the mastery. She looked up to my face and said:

"'Are you the man that preached last night and said that Christ could save to the uttermost?'

"'Yes.'

"'Well, I was there, and I want you to come right down to my house and try to save my poor father."

"'What's the matter with your father?'

"He's a very good father when he don't drink. He's out of work and he drinks awfully. He's almost killed my poor mother; but if Jesus can save to the uttermost, He can save him. And I want you to come right to our house now."

"I took my hat and followed my little guide who trotted on before, halting as she turned the corners to see that I was coming. Oh, what a miserable den her home was! A low, dark, underground room, the floor all slush and mud—not a chair, table, or bed to be seen. A bitter cold night and not a spark of fire on the hob and the room not only cold but dark. In the corner on a little dirty straw, lay a woman. Her head was bound up, and she was moaning as if in agony. As we darkened the doorway a feeble voice said: 'O, my child! my child! why have you brought a stranger into this horrible place?' Her story was a sad one, but soon told. Her husband, out of work, maddened with drink and made desperate, had stabbed her because she did not provide him with a supper that was not in the house. He was then upstairs and she was expecting every moment that he would come down and complete the bloody work he had begun. While the conversation was going on the fiend made his appearance. A fiend he looked. He brandished the knife, still wet with the blood of his wife.

"The missionary, like the man among the tombs, had himself belonged to the desperate classes. He was converted at the mouth of a coal-pit. He knew the disease and the remedy—knew how to handle a man on the borders of delirium tremens.

"Subdued by the tender tones, the mad man calmed down, and took a seat on a box. But the talk was interrupted by the little girl, who approached the missionary, and said:

"Don't talk to father; it won't do any good. If talking would have saved him, he would have been saved long ago. Mother has talked to him so much and so good. You must ask Jesus, who saves to the uttermost, to save my poor father."

"Rebuked by the faith of the little girl, the missionary and the miserable sinner knelt down together. He prayed as he never prayed before; he entreated and interceded, in tones so tender and fervent that it melted the desperate man, who cried for mercy. And mercy came. He bowed in penitence before the Lord, and lay down that night on his pallet of straw a pardoned soul.

"Relief came to that dwelling. The wife was lifted from her dirty couch, and her home was made comfortable. On Sunday, the reformed man took the hand of his little girl and entered the infant class, to learn something about the Savior, 'who saves to the uttermost.' He entered upon a new life. His reform was thorough. He found good employment, for when sober he was an excellent workman; and next to his Saviour, he blesses God for the faith of his little girl, who believed in a Savior able to save to the uttermost all that come unto God by him."

A Wonderful Children's Meeting.

Several years ago, when residing at G., we became acquainted with Sister W.— who was especially fond of children. Her own were grown, and desiring to make a home for some homeless child, she went to the county farm, where there were several, in search of one. Among the children there she found a beautiful little bright-eyed girl, about nine years old, whose name was Ida. Her heart went out to her at once and she expressed to the lady in charge her desire to take Ida, and her willingness to care for her as she would if she were her own child. But the matron said: "Oh, you have no idea what a terrible child she is! We can do nothing with her, she is stubborn and has an awful temper and it is impossible to control her. We are intending to send her to the Girl's Reform School." Sister W.,—who was an earnest christian, was surprised but not discouraged. She could not bear the thought of such a little child being sent to such a place and so she said to the matron: "Well, I'd like to take her with me and see if I cannot help her to be good." "Well," said the matron, "You can try her if you want to, but you will be glad to bring her back again." Acting upon this permission, Sister W.—talked with Ida and easily gained her consent to go with her. Not many days had passed be-

She had not talked long until nearly every child in the room was in tears.

fore she found that there was considerable reason for what the matron had said. Ida was hard to control and at times became terribly angry without cause; but Sister W.— prayed for her and dealt patiently and tenderly with her and told her how Jesus loved her, and would help her to be good if she would only give him her heart. Her prayers and loving labor were not in vain and it was not very long until little Ida was converted. The change was so great that all who were with her could plainly see that Jesus had indeed given her a new heart.

Soon after this we had charge of a children's meeting held in a mission hall in G.—. Among the children gathered there were many of the worst boys in town. Little Ida was present. We knew how much Jesus had done for her and felt led of the Spirit to ask her to lead the meeting. She looked up at us much surprised but her little heart was full of the love of God and she consented to do the best she could. Words cannot describe what followed. In tears, Ida told, in her own touching way, how Jesus had saved her—just what a naughty girl she had been before she was converted, but how Jesus had "taken the angry all away" and given her a new heart so that she loved everybody and loved to do what was right. Then she plead [sic] with them to give their hearts to God and told them how Jesus died on the cross for them and how He loved them and wanted to save them. She had not talked long until nearly every child in the room was in tears; and how shall we describe that touching scene? We had an altar service. Ida knelt with those who were seeking and prayed for them and told them how to find Jesus; and right there many were converted and gave bright clear testimonies that their sins were forgiven and Jesus had given them new hearts. Thus did God that day honor a little girl's testimony and exhortation and fulfill his own work, "A little child shall lead them." Very often do we call to mind that scene, and we find it one of the sweetest of the memories of years of evangelistic work.—Editor.

"They Are Not Strangers, Mamma"

Not long ago I stood by the death-bed of a little girl. From her birth she had been afraid of death. Every fiber of her body and soul recoiled from the thought of it, "Don't let me die," she said; "don't let me die. Hold me fast. Oh, I can't go!"

"Jennie," I said, "You have two little brothers in the other world, and there are thousands of tender-hearted people over there, who will love you and take care of you."

But she cried out again despairingly: "Don't let me go they are strangers over there." She was a little country girl, strong limbed, fleet of foot, tanned in the face; she was raised on the frontier, the fields were her home. In vain we tried to reconcile her to the death that was inevitable. "Hold me fast," she cried; "don't let me go." But even as she was pleading, her little hands relaxed their clinging hold from my waist, and lifted themselves eagerly aloft; lifted themselves with such straining effort, that they lifted the wasted little body from its reclining

position among the pillows. Her face was turned upward, but it was her eyes that told the story. They were filled with the light of Divine recognition. They saw something plainly that we could not see; and they grew brighter and brighter, and her little hand quivered in eagerness to go, where strange portals had opened upon her astonished vision. But even in that supreme moment she did not forget to leave a word of comfort for those who would gladly have died in her place: "Mamma," she was saying, "mamma, they are not strangers. I'm not afraid." And every instant the light burned more gloriously in her blue eyes, till at last it seemed as if her soul leaped forth upon its radiant waves; and in that moment her trembling form relapsed among its pillows and she was gone. — *Chicago Woman's World.*

Jessie Finding Jesus.

A little girl in a wretched tenement in New York stood by her mother's death-bed, and heard her last words: "Jessie, find Jesus."

When her mother was buried, her father took to drink, and Jessie was left to such care as a poor neighbor could give her. One day she wandered off unmissed, with a little basket in her hand, and tugged through one street after another, not knowing where she went. She had started out to find Jesus. At last she stopped from utter weariness, in front of a saloon. A young man staggered out of the door, and almost stumbled over her. He uttered passionately the name of Him whom she was seeking.

"Where is He?" she inquired eagerly.

He looked at her in amazement.

"What did you say?" he asked.

"Will you please tell me where Jesus Christ is? for I must find Him" — this time with great earnestness.

The young man looked at her curiously for a minute without speaking, and then his face sobered; and he said in a broken, husky voice, hopelessly: "I don't know, child; I don't know where he is."

At length the little girl's wanderings brought her to the park. A woman, evidently a Jewess, was leaning against the railing, looking disconsolately at the green grass and the trees.

Jessie went up to her timidly. "Perhaps she can tell me where He is," was the child's thought. In a low, hesitating voice, she asked the woman: "Do you know Jesus Christ?"

The Jewess turned fiercely to face her questioner and in a tone of suppressed passion, exclaimed: "Jesus Christ is dead!" Poor Jessie trudged on, but soon a rude boy jostled against her, and snatching her basket from her hand, threw it into the street.

Crying, she ran to pick it up. The horses of a passing street-car trampled her under their feet — and she knew no more till she found herself stretched on a hospital bed.

When the doctors came that night, they knew she could

not live until morning. In the middle of the night, after she had been lying very still for a long time, apparently asleep, she suddenly opened her eyes and the nurse, bending over her, heard her whisper, while her face lighted up with a smile that had some of heaven's own gladness in it: "O Jesus, I have found you at last!"

Then the tiny lips were hushed, but the questioning spirit had received an answer. — *Selected*.

"I'll Never Steal Again—If Father Kills Me For It."

A friend of mine, seeking for objects of charity, got into the room of a tenement house. It was vacant. He saw a ladder pushed through the ceiling. Thinking that perhaps some poor creature had crept up there, he climbed the ladder, drew himself up through the hole and found himself under the rafters. There was no light but that which came through a bull's-eye in the place of a tile. Soon he saw a heap of chips and shavings, and on them a boy about ten years old.

"Boy, what are you doing there?"

"Hush! don't tell anybody—please, sir."

"What are you doing here?"

"Don't tell anybody, sir; I'm hiding."

"What are you hiding from?"

"Don't tell anybody, if you please, sir.

"Where's your mother?"

"Mother is dead."

"Where's your father?"

"Hush! don't tell him! don't tell him! but look here!"

He turned himself on his face and through the rags of his jacket and shirt my friend saw the boy's flesh was bruised and the skin broken.

"Why, my boy, who beat you like that?"

"Father did, sir."

"What did your father beat you like that for?"

"Father got drunk, sir, and beat me 'cos I wouldn't steal."

"Did you ever steal?"

"Yes, sir, I was a street thief once."

"And why don't you steal any more?"

"Please, sir, I went to the mission school, and they told me there of God and of Heaven and of Jesus, and they taught me, 'Thou shalt not steal,' and I'll never steal again, if father kills me for it. But, please sir, don't tell him."

"My boy, you must not stay here; you will die. Now you wait patiently here for a little time; I'm going away to see a lady. We will get a better place for you than this."

"Thank you sir, but please, sir, would you like to hear me sing a little hymn?"

Bruised, battered, forlorn, friendless, motherless, hiding away from an infuriated father, he had a little hymn to sing.

"Yes. I will hear you sing your little hymn."

He raised himself on his elbow and then sang:

"Gentle Jesus, meek and mild,
Look upon a little child;
Suffer me to come to Thee.
Fain would I to Thee be brought,
Gracious Lord, forbid it not;
In the kingdom of Thy grace
Give a little child a place."

"That's the little hymn, sir; Good-bye."

The gentleman went away, came back again in less than two hours and climbed the ladder. There were the chips and there was the little boy with one hand by his side and the other tucked in his bosom underneath the little ragged shirt—dead.—*John B. Gough.*

Six Months' Record.

[The incidents in the following little sketch were given me by Rev. Dr.
A. J. Gordon, during his stay with us at Northfield, Mass. He afterwards
kindly gave permission to have them used, if it was so desired. His recent
departure is to so very many a most personal loss, that any reminiscence
of him will be welcome.—L. C. W.]

Very tiny and pale the little girl looked as she stood
before those three grave and dignified gentlemen. She
had been ushered into Rev. Dr. Gordon's study, where he
was holding counsel with two of his deacons, and now,
upon inquiry into the nature of her errand, a little shyly
preferred the request to be allowed to become a member
of his church.

"You are quite too young to join church," said one of
the deacons, "you had better run home, and let us talk to
your mother."

She showed no sign of running, however, as her wist-
ful blue eyes traveled from one face to another of the three
gentlemen sitting in their comfortable chairs; she only
drew a step nearer to Dr. Gordon. He arose, and with
gentle courtesy that ever marked him, placed her in a
small chair close beside himself.

"Now, my child, tell me your name, and where you live."

"Winnie Lewis, sir, and I live on —— Street. I go to Sunday school."

"You do; and who is your teacher?"

"Miss ——. She is very good to me."

"And you want to join my church?"

The child's face glowed as she leaned eagerly toward him, clasping her hands, but all she said was, "Yes, sir."

"She cannot be more than six years old," said one of the deacons, disapprovingly.

Dr. Gordon said nothing, but quietly regarded the small, earnest face, now becoming a little down cast.

"I am nine years old; older than I look," she said.

"It is not usual for us to admit anyone so young to membership," he said, thoughtfully, "We never have done so; still —."

"It may make an undesireable precedent," remarked the other deacon.

The Doctor did not seem to hear, as he asked, "You know what joining the church is, Winnie?"

"Yes, sir;" and she answered a few questions that proved she comprehended the meaning of the step she wished to take. She had slipped off her chair, and now stood close to Dr. Gordon's knee.

"You said, last Sabbath, sir, that the lambs should be in the fold —."

"I did," he answered, with one of his own lovely smiles. "It is surely not for us to keep them out. Go home now, my child. I will see your friends and arrange to take you into membership very soon."

The cloud lifted from the child's face, and her expression, as she passed through the door he opened for her, was one of entire peace.

Inquiries made of Winnie's Sabbath School teacher proving satisfactory, she was baptized the following week, and except for occasional information from Miss —— that she was doing well, Dr. Gordon heard no more of her for six months.

Then he was summoned to her funeral.

It was one of June's hottest days, and as the Doctor made his way along the narrow street on which Winnie had lived, he wished for a moment, that he had asked his assistant to come instead of himself, but as he neared the house, the crowd filled him with wonder; progress was hindered, and as perforce he paused for a moment, his eye fell on a crippled lad crying bitterly as he sat on a low doorstep.

"Did you know Winnie Lewis, my lad?" he asked.

"Know her, is it sir? Never a week passed but what she came twice or thrice with a picture or book, mayhaps an apple for me, an' it's owing to her an' no clargy at all that I'll ever follow her blessed footsteps to heaven. She'd read me from her own Bible wheniver she came, an' now she's gone there'll be none at all to help me, for mother's dead an' dad's drunk, an' the sunshine's gone from Mike's sky intoirely with Winnie, sir."

A burst of sobs choked the boy; Bro. Gordon passed on, after promising him a visit very soon, and made his way through the crowd of tear-stained, sorrowful faces. The Doctor came to a stop again on the narrow passageway of the little house. A woman stood beside him drying her fast falling tears while a wee child hid his face in her skirts and wept.

"Was Winnie a relative of yours?" the Doctor asked.

"No, sir; but the blessed child was at our house constantly, and when Bob here was sick she nursed and tended him, and her hymns quieted him when nothing else seemed to do it. It was just the same with all the neighbors. She took tracts to them all and has prayed with them ever since she was converted, which was three years ago, when she was but six years of age, sir. What she's

"Mother, mother come away," said a young man, putting his arm round her to lead her back. "You'll see her again." "I know, I know: she said she'd wait for me at the gate,"

been to us all no one but the Lord will ever know and now she lies there."

Recognized at last, Dr. Gordon was led to the room where the child lay at rest, looking almost younger than when he had seen her in his study six months before. An old bent woman was crying aloud by the coffin.

"I never thought she'd go afore I did. She used regular to read an' sing to me every evening, an' it was her talk an' prayers that made a Christian of me: you could a'most go to heaven on one of her prayers."

"Mother, mother come away," said a young man, putting his arm around her to lead her back. "You'll see her again."

"I know, I know: she said she'd wait for me at the gate," she sobbed as she followed him; "but I miss her sore now."

"It's the old lady as Mrs. Lewis lived with, sir," said a young lad standing next to Dr. Gordon, as one and another still pressed up towards the little casket, for a last look at the beloved face. "She was a Unitarian, but she could not hold out against Winnie's prayers and pleadings to love Jesus, and she's been trusting in Him now for quite awhile. A mighty good thing it is, too."

"You are right, my lad," replied the Doctor, "Do you trust Him too?"

"Winnie taught me, sir," the lad made answer, and sudden tears filled his eyes.

A silence fell on those assembled, and, marveling at such testimony, Dr. Gordon proceeded with the service, feeling as if there was little more he could say of one whose deeds thus spoke for her. Loving hands had laid flowers all around the child who had led them. One tiny lassie placed a dandelion in the small waxen fingers and now stood, abandoned to grief beside the still form that bore the impress of absolute purity. The service over, again and again was the coffin lid waved back by some one longing for another look, and they seemed as if they could not let her go.

The next day a good-looking man came to Dr. Gordon's house and was admitted into his study.

"I am Winnie's uncle, sir," he said simply. "She never rested till she made me promise to join the church, and I've come."

"Will you tell me about it, my friend?" said Dr. Gordon.

"Well, you see, sir, it was this way. Winnie always had been uncommonly fond of me, and so was I of her," — his voice broke a little — "and I'd never joined the Church, never felt, as I believed, quite right. Yet I knew her religion was true enough, and a half hour before she died she had the whole family with her, telling them she was going to Jesus, and she took my hand between her little ones and said, 'Uncle John, you will love Jesus and meet me in Heaven, won't you?' What could I do? It broke me all up, and I've come to ask you, sir; what to do so's to keep my promise to Winnie, for she was an angel if there ever was one. Why, sir, we were all sitting with her in the dark, and there was a light about that child as though it shone from Heaven. We all noticed it, every one of us, and when she drew her last breath and left us, the radiance went too; it was gone, quite gone."

The man wept like a child, and for a minute Dr. Gordon did not speak. Within a month Winnie's uncle was baptized in the church, thoroughly converted, and a sincere follower of Christ. In the evening after this baptism, Dr. Gordon sat resting, in his study, thinking of his little child member. "It is truly a wonderful record! Would we had more like her. Why do we not take the children into membership, letting them feel that they are really one with us? We need their help fully as much as they need our's [sic]. 'Take heed that ye despise not one of these little ones; for I say unto you, That in Heaven their angels do always behold the face of my Father which is in Heaven." — *L. C. W. Copyright by J. B. Wood, 1895.*

A Child's Faith.

Johnny Hall was a poor boy. His mother worked hard for their daily bread. "Please give me something to eat, for I am very hungry," he said to her one evening.

His mother let the work that she was sewing fall upon her knees, and drew Johnny toward her. As she kissed him the tears fell fast on his face, while she said, "Johnny, my dear, I have not a penny in the world. There is not a morsel of bread in the house, and I cannot give you any to-night."

Johnny did not cry when he heard this. He was only a little fellow, but he had learned the lesson of trusting in God's promises. He had great faith in the sweet words of Jesus when he said, "Whatsoever ye shall ask the Father in my name he will give it you."

"Never mind, mamma; I shall soon be asleep, and then I shall not feel hungry. But you must sit here and sew,

hungry and cold. Poor mamma!" he said, as he threw his arms, round her neck and kissed her many times to comfort her.

Then he knelt down at his mother's knee, to say his prayers after her. They said "Our Father," till they came to the petition, "Give us this day our daily bread." The way in which his mother said these words made Johnny's heart ache. He stopped and looked at her, and repeated with his eyes full of tears. "Give us this day our daily bread."

When they got through he looked at his mother and said, "Now mother, do not be afraid. We shall never be hungry any more. God is our father. He has promised to hear us, and I am sure he will."

Then he went to bed. Before midnight he woke up, while his mother was still at work, and asked if the bread had come yet. She said "No; but I am sure it will come."

In the morning, before Johnny was awake, a gentleman called who wanted his mother to come to his house and take charge of his two motherless children. She agreed to go. He left some money with her. She went out at once to buy some things for breakfast; and when Johnny awoke, the bread was there, and all that he needed!

Johnny is now a man, but he has never wanted bread from that day; and whenever he was afraid since then, he has remembered God's promises, and trusted in him. — *Lutheran Herald*

Triumphant Death of a Little Child.

Some years ago we knew a Brother and Sister G., who told us of the remarkable experience of their little girl, only seven years old, who had a short time ago gone home to heaven. The parents were devoted Christians who had taught their children to love and honor

"I have been in heaven all night. My room is full of angels and Jesus is here."

God. During little Ella's illness she manifested wonderful patience and told of her love for Jesus. The morning she died she called her papa and mama to her side and said: "I have been in heaven all night. My room is full of angels and Jesus is here. I'm going to heaven." Then she asked them to promise to meet her there. As soon as they could control their feelings they made her the promise. Then she kissed them and called for her little brother and sister and other friends. She talked with each one in turn, telling them in substance, the same she had told her papa and mama, asking each one to make her the same promise, and kissing each one good-bye. That was a touching scene. Those who were there said it seemed more like heaven than earth to be in her presence. In the midst of many tears all promised her they would surely meet her in that bright beautiful home to which she was going. Just before she died she asked her mama to dress her in white and also to dress her doll in white and put it by her side in her coffin. Then she folded her own little hands and closed her eyes and said, "Jesus is calling me and I must go now. Good-bye," and she was gone.

Little Ella's death was glorious and she is not the only one that has left us such bright, joyous testimony. We have ourselves known of many children and older ones who had quite similar experiences. And though we may not all see, before we die, all that Ella saw, if we love Jesus and do what he asks us to, he will surely fulfil to each of us his promise: "I go to prepare a place for you. And if I go and prepare a place for you, I will come again, and receive you unto myself; that where I am, there you may be also." — *Editor*

The Child's Prayer.

Into her chamber went
    A little girl one day,
And by a chair she knelt,
    And thus began to pray:—
"Jesus, my eyes I close,
    Thy form I cannot see;
If thou art near me, Lord,
    I pray thee to speak to me."
A still small voice she heard within her soul—
"What is it child? I hear thee; tell the whole."

"I pray thee, Lord," she said,
    "That Thou wilt condescend
To tarry in my heart
    And ever be my friend.
The path of life is dark,
    I would not go astray;
O, let me have Thy hand
    To lead me in the way."
"Fear not; I will not leave thee, child, alone."
She thought she felt a soft hand press her own.

"They tell me, Lord, that all
   The living pass away;
The aged soon must die,
   And even children may.
O, let my parents live
   Till I a woman grow;
For if they die, what can
   A little orphan do?"
"Fear not, my child; whatever ill may come
I'll not forsake thee till I bring thee home."

Her little prayer was said,
   And from her chamber now
She passed forth with the light
   Of heaven upon her brow.
"Mother, I've seen the Lord,
   His hand in mine I felt,
And, O, I heard Him say,
   As by my chair I knelt:—
"Fear not, my child; whatever ill may come
I'll not forsake thee till I bring thee home."

                                        —*Evangelist*

MEMBERS OF SCHMUL'S WESLEYAN BOOK CLUB
BUY THESE OUTSTANDING BOOKS AT 40% OFF
THE RETAIL PRICE

Join Schmul's Wesleyan Book Club by calling toll-free:

800-S$_7$P$_7$B$_2$O$_6$O$_6$K$_5$S$_7$

Put a discount Christian bookstore in your
own mailbox

Visit us on the Internet at
www.wesleyanbooks.com

Schmul Publishing Company | PO Box 776 | Nicholasville, KY | 40340 | www.wesleyanbooks.com

www.ingramcontent.com/pod-product-compliance
Lightning Source LLC
Chambersburg PA
CBHW061833040426
42447CB00012B/2942